A Line in the Sand

The true story of a Marine's experience on the front lines of the Gulf War

Robert A. Serocki Jr.

A Line In The Sand

Copyright © 2006 Robert Serocki

All rights reserved. No part of this book may be copied or reproduced in any manner without written permission from the author.

Layout & design: The Agrell Group
www.theagrellgroup.com

One World Press
1042 Willow Creek Road
Prescott, AZ 86301
800-250-8171
www.OneWorldPress.com

This book was printed in the U.S.A. on recycled paper using soy ink.

ISBN: 0-9742014-9-9

06 07 08 09 10   5 4 3 2 1

This book is dedicated to my Grandfather. He was the strongest, smartest man I have ever met. Thank you for always being there for me and for all of your advice.
I love you and may you rest in peace sir!

This book is the story of the events, which took place during the Gulf War. I have undoubtedly forgotten some events and experiences. Others, I remember rather vividly. I also have changed people's names in order to protect their anonymity.

*"Oh mother, tell your children not to do what
I have done and spend your life in sin and misery,
in the house of the rising sun."*

Eric Burdon and The Animals

Surviving a war is the smallest of battles a soldier must face, when left with the never ending war he must fight in his mind. It is a much graver wound to survive, than to die. He who dies is liberated from war's confine. A warrior who lives through such a tribulation must re-walk the path he has already once traveled. Hence, fighting the war for eternity!

Robert A. Serocki Jr.
July 21, 2000

AKNOWLEDGEMENTS

First of all, I would like to thank Rodger Lidman for his encouragement and his comments on the rough draft of this book. I would also like to thank Todd Bostwick for all of his encouragement and support throughout the production of my book. A special thank you to my friends and family, Tom and Carol Shortland, Bob Serocki, Dennis and Sandy Grenier, Gary Grenier, Gerald and Bernice Grenier, Jeff and Wendy Low, Lee White and Eric Fincher, for all of your help and support from the time I came home from the war until now. Another special thanks goes out to the band, Al Rotten, Mitch Vicious, Duppie, The Viking, Paul, Vivian and Guy, Susie, and the Pontiff, for accepting me just the way I was and for just being there. Thank you to Stacey Ray for several reviews of a rough draft of this book, your efforts have only enhanced its quality. A very special thank you goes to Marlo Van Horn, for all of your help and understanding over the course of the five years we had together. I admire your strength, courage, and compassion when you helped me deal with my problems, even though you did not know what I was going through. There is not a single day that goes by that I do not think of you and smile. Finally, I would like to thank Laura Andrew for the final edit of this book.

INTRODUCTION

This book is a true account of my experience as a Marine in the Gulf War. I decided to tell my story in hopes of developing, in the reader, a deeper respect for America's veterans by revealing the extreme mental and physical sacrifices a soldier must make during war. I want to show how our own government, while fulfilling our duty, treated us, how people get through such experiences and what those people do to keep their sanity.

For me it was music and religion. I lived vicariously in the songs; they allowed me to mentally release pent up emotions and often, at times, the music would take me away to a place where there was no danger. Belief in a supreme being helped me to also cast away my fears. I had God to confide in and it was a way to help make me feel like I had some control over my destiny. It also helped me to accept death.

I served two tours in the Gulf War. Marines did not have the luxury of knowing that when our tour of duty was over we could go home. We were there for the duration, no matter how long that took. As the Commandant of the Marine Corps put it so gracefully in the Saudi desert on a blistering hot October day, "Your head and your ass are in my corner and you will go home when I say you can go home!" War is pure hell, no matter how quickly it ends or how long it lasts.

Ever since I came home from the Gulf War I have had to deal with hearing things like "Oh, that was an easy war" or "They didn't even fight, you guys had it easy." People kept telling me "Oh, that wasn't a real war." Compared to other wars, such as World War I, World War II, Korea, and more recently Vietnam, the loss of life, on our side, was far less. However, no war is easy and losing one life, let alone a few hundred, is one too many. I hope to dispel these perceptions and show what really happened in the Gulf War. The fact of the matter is, as General Norman Schwartzkopf put it, "It's not that the Iraqi's didn't fight, it's that our troops are just that damn good!"

I hope to show the realities of war, which can be quite unnerving and gut wrenching. Realities that were so painful they have forced grown men to wound and even kill themselves just to escape. Memories that cause them to do drugs, drink and completely defile themselves for a release from the pain, if only for a few hours. I want to reveal the stark differences between what really happens in war and what is reported to the American people. We all had to change and adapt to our situation overseas in order to survive, greatly changing all of our lives once we returned home. As the Marine Corps always says, "Adapt, overcome, and improvise!" In the past I had to apply this esoteric phrase to many enigmatic cycles of my life in order to overcome them.

Back when I was contemplating writing this book I was taken by a quote from the movie *Platoon*, by Oliver Stone. At the end of the movie, Charlie Sheen's character reflects on his experiences and says, "Those of us who make it home have an obligation to rebuild again and to teach the world

Introduction

what we know." With this book, I hope to achieve this. Those of us, who do make it, have made it for a reason. I think, for me, that reason is the one so poignantly stated above; I have an obligation to rebuild and to teach the world what I know.

Finally, I have included most of the letters I wrote home while I was in the Gulf War. They contain many grammatical errors and misspellings. This is because I included them in this book exactly the way I wrote them in 1990/1991.

1

IF I LAUGH

*If I laugh just a little bit, maybe I can forget the chance
that I didn't have to know you and live in peace, in
peace.... If I laugh just a little bit, maybe I can recall
the way I used to be before you and sleep at night and
dream.*

by Cat Stevens

Evening has descended upon me as I rise from my chair in front of my computer. I have been typing all day and now that the sun has begun its retreat, the soft glow of my computer screen illuminates the dusk engulfed room. I hit the save icon on the screen and walk out of the room into the family room.

I decide that I deserve a reward. I walk over to my armoire and open it. Inside I keep all of my beer, wine, whiskey glasses, various bottles of booze, and assorted bottles of wine. I decided to make a martini, so I search for my bottle of Polish vodka.

As I grab the bottle and scan its label my mind harkens back to a time when my life was nothing but pain. It was a time when booze was my aspirin, my cure all. It cured pain, depression, loneliness and self-pity. It made me feel euphoric. It became my happy pill. We used to call it combat cough syrup in the Marines. Now I am able to enjoy fine liquors, beer and wine instead of just merely punishing myself with them. Or, I do not imbibe them at all. I have overcome that battle. It was one battle in the years of battles that I had fought with myself, from the time I came home from the Gulf War, until now.

Tonight, I will make myself a vodka martini, watch the sun set and relax. I have finally overcome the biggest battle thus far in my civilian life. I have written the story of my experience as a Marine on the front line of the Gulf War. In order to do this, I had to re-live the entire war. I had to replay its events; rank stenches of burning, rotting flesh, searing pain, utter misery, revolting scenes of disarticulated pieces of body parts, my comrades full of holes, covered in blood and bandages so that they resemble patch work quilts. It unfolds, in my mind, as though it were a movie playing before my very eyes.

I have finally forced myself to face it. I have had much encouragement from my bosses at work, family and friends. It was the last piece of my puzzle. I have finally found the last piece making it complete. I feel whole again. I no longer feel as if my life and my body are pieces scattered all over a coffee table just waiting to be put back together. Since the war, it has taken me twelve years and the many battles to fix me, to make me complete again. This last battle, writing my story, has taken me nearly four years to complete.

I grab the bottle and my martini shaker and stroll into the kitchen where I grab some ice. I mix up the martini, pour it into the glass and add some olive juice and three olives. I grab my once magical elixir and walk back into the family room. I pulled my sofa chair in front of the window and I finally sit down to relax.

I take a sip of the chilled drink and my chest is overcome by a warm sensation as the alcohol burns its way down my esophagus and into my gut. With a few more sips, I begin to feel the tension in my extremities dissipate. It almost feels like the blood is again rushing back into my fingers and toes. I survey the landscape in front of my window. Mountains surround my house as though they were walls around a fortress. Yet, I am taken with the openness of the desert that flows up to my porch like the froth of an ocean wave on the beach.

I watch rabbits dart back and forth across the road to nibble on the sweet leaves of the mesquite trees dangling just above the desert floor as though God was teasing the hungry creatures. I watch doves and gamble quail race around with their topknots bobbing as they peck the ground for seeds to nourish their hungry souls.

The sun is now setting. It is descending behind the mountains to rest for the night. It will then rise again tomorrow to start a new day. I think to myself, "How fortuitous is this? The sun rises and sets, thus ending a phase and a new one begins." Profoundly, I am overcome by this event. This is the same exact spot my life is in at the same exact moment as the sun and the rest of the world.

I begin to cry. I cry for what seems like hours. It is as if my top has finally blown and everything is just spilling out. I feel like a Coke bottle that has been shaken profusely and subsequently opened as all of my tension foams out into my hands. I begin to shake and I take several deep breaths. I take another sip of my martini and tell myself that everything will be ok. "This is good. I need to let it all out."

I think about what I really wanted. I really yearned for someone to say thank you. I would look at my phone and wait. It did not ring. I found myself waiting for the phone to ring on Veteran's day; it never has rung. I waited by the phone on the Fourth of July, but the phone did not ring. I waited for those calls for twelve years. I decide this is ok because I made my sacrifice out of the goodness of my heart, not to selfishly expect anything for it.

I think about all the times that I have drank myself into oblivion while the rest of the world moved on. I sat there trapped in time. I sat there trapped in a war. No one wanted to talk to me. No one liked me. To them, I was a crazy psychopathic war machine. I used to kill people for a living. They hypothesized about how I could not be right in the head. Therefore, I was avoided. It was like I had a plague. It was like my face had been so grotesquely disfigured and repulsive that no one could look at me. They were wrong! However, I cannot get mad. Because of me, and thousands of other forgotten people like me, these loathsome human beings have the freedom to think such sophomoric and trite things.

I think about how I existed in a drunken stupor, in a euphoric state of mind while the rest of the world thought it ok to carry on with their lives. No one checked on me to see if I was ok. No one cared. The world was safe for them now. Therefore, I was no longer needed. But you see, I am needed. I have a message to give.

I remember how I would think about all of my friends and how successful they have become. I thought about how they all have beautiful homes, wives, children and more than one car. I would then look around my humble surroundings.

I would notice that my floor was concrete, my roof leaked, my cupboard doors were falling off of the hinges, my furniture did not match, my truck had over one hundred thousand miles on it, and how I could not turn on the heat or air because it cost too much.

Yet, they called me when they had problems and I helped them. I made them laugh. I made them realize they really had nothing to complain about. I am an example to them of how bad off they could be. They can say, "at least I am not like Robert was."

They tell me now that I am the glue that holds everyone together. They tell me they admire the fact that I am such a happy go lucky guy no matter what happens to me. They never realized that I used to hurt inside. I was a house built on a disarticulated foundation of pain and suffering. They all had something or someone to help them. I had nothing.

I finally quit crying. So I decided to call my mother and tell her about my accomplishment. She has received many phone calls from me. I love my mother. She always listens. She lets me spill my guts. My mother is my crutch. She helps me work through my problems and at the same time she is careful enough to let me do the work so that I may learn. She is an amazing woman full of courage and strength. I have heard people say that before you come into this world you pick your parents. I must have done this because there is no way fate could have picked a better mother.

I remember after my parents got divorced and we lived in Arizona and my father lived in Michigan. My mother and step-father had my dad fly to Arizona to visit us kids. My mother let him stay at our house. I think to myself how uncomfortable all three of them must have felt. Yet, they did not show it. They just made sure us kids were well taken care of as they put our needs well above their own.

She answered the phone and I told her what I had done. She told me she was happy that I wrote the book and that process would be good therapy for me. She told me that it would help me to release the tumultuous emotions that I had been harboring for years. I begin to cry again. The memories of my life flow back into my mind at rapid speed. My head feels like a tape that is being played at high speed so the people on it sound like they have inhaled large doses of helium. My mother calms me down by making me laugh. We hang up the phone. I make sure I call my mother every day now.

The sun is almost gone. Everything is orange, blue, pink and purple. I am reminded of my fishing trips with my father at the age of three or four. I remember standing in the kitchen. It was still dark outside. Dad was making bologna and mustard sandwiches on Wonder bread. He then filled up the thermos with coffee. He wishes me good morning and we grab our food, drinks and gear. We get into the car and drive off. The sun then began to rise and the morning looked just like it did now, outside of my window.

The morning was fresh and new. The day held the fresh promise of catching stringers of fish. I was excited. Some days we would catch nothing, others we would catch a lot. One time I even caught a Northern Pike that was as big as my three-year-old body. The fish had scared me so much that I ran up to the bow of the boat and would not come back down to the aft of the boat as long as the fish was there. After all, his teeth were much larger than mine.

The fish is now stuffed and hanging in my office. I look at it and smile. There were good days and bad, disappointments and joys. I then realize that is exactly what life is like. Yes, life is just like the rising sun with its cycles of beginnings and endings.

I begin to think about all of the beginnings and endings of the cycles of my life, childhood, school, boot camp, war and the rebuilding of my life. I feel like I am coming full circle. I feel like now, I can begin the cycle of enjoying my life and living it to its fullest potential. It is now dark, pitch black and I cannot see a thing outside the window except my streetlight. All appears to be still, calm, serene and asleep.

Then I begin to remember three dreams I continuously had while I was in high school. I would dream that I was in the Revolutionary War and that I was running from these soldiers and I lay down behind a hill. I pointed my musket at them. Just as I was ready to pull my trigger, I hear a crack above my right ear and I get shot in my chest and the bullet comes out my back. I feel the searing pain and burning from the hot bullet. I then die.

The second dream that I would always have was about the Civil War. I never could remember what side I was on. I fought a battle in an area that was filled with pine trees and sandstone. I was running from some men who were chasing me during a big bloody battle. I ran and hid in a compartment under the wagon that was used to store luggage. A soldier from the other side entered the wagon and opened the floorboard and buried his bayonet into my chest and it poked out my back. I then died.

The third dream that I had was that I was in the Vietnam War. I was a Sergeant. I was walking through an area of tall brown grass. The tree line was a distance off, but all around us. It was just my radioman and myself. Everyone else had been killed. It began to rain profusely. I spotted a white house with a thatch roof. I tell the radioman that we are going to go into the house to get out of the rain for a while. Just as I say that, I hear a crack and I am shot in the back and the bullet comes out my chest and I die from bleeding to death.

As I recall these dreams I think about how I ended up in each one of those dreams and how I have been to war now and I am still alive. I ponder the fact that I no longer have these dreams. I also contemplate the fact that I now have problems with my chest and back in the same locations that I got shot in the dreams.

A song crosses my mind at this moment. I mumble the words to myself as though I am agreeing with their message of hope.

> *Carry on my wayward son. There will be peace when you are done. Lay your weary head to rest. Don't you cry no more.*
>
> Kansas

I get up from the chair. I look at my half drunken martini and I grab it and stroll into the kitchen. Setting the glass on the counter, I look up to the ceiling and I say a prayer to God. I thank him for giving me the strength, courage and perseverance to make it through everything that has happened to me and for being able to complete this most recent of tasks. I promise him that I will not fail him and I will tell the world my story and that perhaps someone will learn from me.

A passage from the Bible then floods into my mind and its words begin to soothe my soul. The words remind me that life has a purpose and faith in God will help you to prevail over what seem like insurmountable situations. The message it gives tells me that all of the experiences we face as human beings are for the purpose of teaching us, so that we may perform the task God requires of us to complete. The passage is from Peter 4:1–12. It reads as follows:

If I Laugh

Therefore, since Christ suffered in his body, arm yourselves also with the same attitude, because he who has suffered in his body is done with sin. As a result, he does not live the rest of his earthly life for evil human desires, but rather for the will of God. For you have spent enough time in the past doing what pagans choose to do—living in debauchery, lust, drunkenness, orgies, carousing and detestable idolatry. They think it strange that you do not plunge with them into the same flood of dissipation, and they heap abuse on you. But they will have to give account to him who is ready to judge the living and the dead. For this is the reason the gospel was preached even to those who are now dead, so that they might be judged according to men in regard to the body, but live according to God in regard to the spirit.

The end of all things is near. Therefore be clear-minded and self-controlled so that you can pray. Above all, love each other deeply, because love covers over a multitude of sins. Offer hospitality to one another without grumbling. Each one should use whatever gift he has received to serve others, faithfully administering God's grace in its various forms.

If anyone speaks, he should do it as one speaking the very words of God. If anyone serves, he should do it with the strength God provides, so that in all things God may be praised through Jesus Christ. To him be the glory and the power for ever and ever. Amen.

I then pick up the martini glass and dump the remaining drink into the sink and I set the glass on the counter.

2

SCHOOL DAYS

> *"Up in the morning and out to school, the teacher is teaching the golden rule, American history and practical math, study real hard hopin to pass, working your fingers right down to the bone, and the guy behind you wont leave you alone....."*
>
> By Chuck Berry

We lived in Sterling Heights Michigan, a suburb of Detroit. I was born on January 30, 1970 in Royal Oak, Michigan. I spent most of my childhood in and around Detroit. My parents divorced when I was ten. A little while after the divorce my mom remarried. At that point I had a mom, step-dad and my dad. From that point on, I spent Wednesdays, Saturdays and Sundays with my dad and the rest of the time with my mother and step-dad.

A Line In the Sand

I was an avid prankster as a little kid and I was also very inquisitive, as are most children. When I was about four years old, I was in the basement, where we kept a fish tank. In it were two fish that I had caught while fishing with my dad on Lake St. Claire. One fish was a Perch and the other was a Large Mouth Bass. I also kept a fresh water clam in the tank. My inquisitive nature took over and I decided to see what the clam looked like inside. So, I took the handle from a paint roller, which was about twelve inches long. The threaded end was covered with metal. I stuck the handle into the tank and hit the clam with it. The clam happened to be located near the glass and one thing led to another. The handle slipped off of the clam and went right through the glass. Water and fish gushed out onto the floor. The bass and the perch were flopping around at my feet. I thought to myself, "Oh man I am in trouble now. How am I going to get out of this one?" I ran up stairs and told my mom the boogeyman did it. Needless to say, when my dad got home, I had to take the boogeyman's butt whooping. It is amazing how things are so simple to children. You are so naïve, everything is new and you see simple solutions to things. You never really think about the bad things until they actually happen to you, the rest of the time you are happy and carefree.

As the days of childhood passed, I got into trouble on more than one occasion. When I was five, I invited three or four of my little buddies in the neighborhood over to my house. We were all sitting on the porch talking, like the adults did on our block. Feeling like an adult I thought, "I should go get some beer for us, like our dads do." When in Rome do as the Romans do, right?

I went down into the basement and got a beer out of the fridge, as I had seen my dad do many times before. Bringing it back out onto the porch, I opened it. The can popped as I pulled the tab back and foam spilled out into my hand. We all passed it around like a soda pop. Meanwhile, my mom got curious as to why all of us boys were so quiet. She knew we were up to something. She found us sitting there on the porch drinking a brew and minding our own business. Needless to say that was the end of that friendly conversation with my buddies.

My friends in the neighborhood and I used to play army every chance we could. In fact, it seems like we passed most of our childhood playing war. We all had toy guns and would get into teams and run around the cul-de-sac, in between houses and pretend we were in big wars. I was always the hero, saving people by taking bullets for them and jumping on grenades. I would always pretend that I got shot in the chest.

Every time my grandmother would visit, my sister and I would get toys. I will never forget seeing that rust colored Dodge Dart with the black top pull up in front of the house. I would get so excited because I knew I was going to Toys 'R' Us to buy more toy army men.

Another event I recall from my childhood, which seemed to permeate every fabric of my entire life, was fighting. I was always getting into fights for one reason or another. On one sunny summer afternoon, while playing with my friends Jack and Curtis, I got into an argument with Curtis who lived next door. He got mad at me and picked up a piece of a rain gutter that ran along the ground away from the house and he started swinging it at me. So, I ran over to the side of his house and grabbed another piece of gutter and swung it back at him splitting his lip wide open.

Blood started gushing out and my friend Jack and I took off running into my backyard. We were going to hop the fence into Jack's yard and hide out at his house. Jack hopped the fence first and then, just as I was about to hop over the top of the fence, my mom yelled for me. "Robert, get your ass over here now!" I knew I was in trouble. I went into the garage where my mother, my friend Curtis and his mother Jan were standing. Curtis held a rag with ice to his lip to stop the bleeding. Jan was chewing my mom out saying, "Look what your son did to my son, he started another fight." My mom then asked Curtis who started it and Curtis admitted that it was his fault. That made Jan awfully uncomfortable and she left.

On yet another occasion during the summer, when I was about five or six, my mom was sitting in the family room watching her favorite soap opera. She had the sliding door to the backyard open. I invited all of my friends over into the backyard to watch as I turned on the hose and squirted my mom through the screen door. She was quite shocked and subsequently, I was too, when dad got home and I got my butt blistered with the belt.

I had nothing to do on another morning that same summer. My mom was still asleep and I was in my pajamas. I went down into the basement and decided that it was time to paint it. I opened a can of white paint and I painted the refrigerator we had down there, the poles that went from the floor to the ceiling, and I painted my fire engine. Then, after I did it, I realized that I would probably get a whooping again. So I went up stairs and decided I would hide and wait it out until the coast was clear.

I crawled under a table in which the sides folded down. My mom finally got up and she went looking for me, she discovered the basement and started screaming my name. I would not budge. I stayed as still as I could be. She came up stairs and saw my feet under the table. She said, "I can see you, get out here right now." I still would not move. I figured if she wanted me she would have to come and get me. She did. Then, when dad got home I got reacquainted with the belt. During my childhood the belt and I got to know each other quite well. I always took my spankings, but I did not like it when people picked on other people, especially my sister.

Anytime someone in the neighborhood would pick on my sister, who is two years younger than me, I would go find them and beat them up. I protected her like she was my own child. It was usually this kid Dillon, from down the street. I called him Dillon, Dillon, watermelon. He did not like that too much. One day my sister, age four, came home crying. I asked her what had happened and she said Dillon had hit her with a tennis racket. I went into the garage and got my mom's blue and white tennis racket and took a stroll down to Dillon's house. When I got there, he and his brother were playing outside. His brother was younger and Dillon was about the same age as me, maybe a little older. I walked up to Dillon and said, "I hear you hit my sister with a tennis racket." Of course, he denied the whole thing. When he did that I took the tennis racket I had and began to pummel Dillon. Then when I had enough of that it broke out into a fistfight. I went home after that and told my sister I took care of it and that Dillon would not be bothering her for a while.

We also had a babysitter who was exceptionally nice, however she irritated me one day and I decided to retaliate. I coaxed my sister into helping me and I organized a plan. We took all of the shoes in the house and lined them up from biggest to smallest behind a wall in the hallway. Then, I went first and my sister followed. "Fire one!" I yelled, as I threw a pair of my dad's size eleven shoes at the babysitter while she watched T.V. My sister repeated my actions and we did it until all the shoes were thrown at her.

The babysitter got up and started chasing me around the coffee table. There was a ceramic fruit bowl my mom had sitting on the end of the coffee table. I still remember it. It was a crème color and had grapes and pears and bananas painted on it. When I noticed the baby sitter gaining on me I gave the bowl a shove onto the floor as I ran by, thinking that would slow her up and give me time to get to my room. However, the bowl broke when it hit the ground and I realized then that I had far bigger problems when my dad got home...the belt! So I quickly changed my strategy and befriended the baby sitter and got her to glue the bowl back together. It was a nice try, but the next morning I got another visit from my old friend the belt.

I also played a lot of sports when I was a child. One of the sports I played was baseball. I had a nickname that everyone used to call me by. They called me the "Hollywood kid". They used to call me this for two reasons. The first reason was, that I was a rather flamboyant dresser as a child. Our team colors were orange and black. The team name was the Bobcats. I used to wear my orange and black hat, orange and black shirt, thick coke bottle glasses with brown plastic frames and a pair of red, white and blue plaid pants and red, white and blue cleats.

The other reason for that nickname was because I was a showboat. One day I hit a home run and as I was rounding third base I looked to the stands and saw my mom jumping up and down screaming and clapping her hands. So, when I crossed home plate, I threw my arms up in the air just as I had seen the professionals do it on T.V.

After that baseball season we moved to a new house in a new neighborhood. I had to start over again with all new kids. I was a little scared, but I soon made new friends. I was eight years old then; the year was 1978.

It was at this age that I became interested in football. I had a talent for it when I was a kid. I used to score touchdowns all the time when I got the ball. I was the team's running back and had some pretty good moves for a kid. I remember two games in particular. I was playing for a team called the Bills. One game, when I caught a pass from the quarterback, I was running so fast down the sideline all I could hear was the wind whistling through my helmet and my breathing. My sister and cousins were the cheerleaders. They were jumping up and down on the sidelines waving their pom-poms. Our team colors were red, white and blue. I got down to the ten-yard line and some kid from the other team caught up with me and yanked my flag, I never quite made it into the end zone that time.

The other game I remember was when I played for the YMCA. We had a good team and our team colors were also red, white and blue. One particular play I got punched in the mouth while I was playing on the defensive line, I got really angry and I told my friend Lonnie what had happened. Lonnie was also on the football team. On the next play the same kid that punched me got the ball. Lonnie tackled the kid and I jumped onto his ribs in retaliation for punching me in the mouth. I thought to myself "I'll teach you for making me bleed." They took him out of the game; it was fourth down. So we got the ball back and on the next play I got the ball and ran all the way down the sidelines, about fifty yards, with my stocking cap over my eyes, for a touch down. Things seemed to be going good. However, shortly thereafter, my life began to metamorphose.

When I was ten, after we lived in our new house for about two years, my parents got divorced. It really was a shock for my sister and I. My mom soon got remarried. So, at ten years old I had my dad, a stepfather and my mother. I had to shuttle back and forth from house to house. I would spend Wednesday's and the weekends with my dad. The rest of the time I would spend with my mother. This is where life really began to change for me. This experience made me a quieter person, and I also harbored a lot of anger because of what happened between my parents. I was angry because I could not have my whole family in one house and spend everyday with both of my parents, I felt cheated. It is a feeling that I had felt numerous times throughout my life.

In the sixth grade things began to change even more for me. Kids started to pick on me and tease me on the playground. They were all getting bigger and I was a skinny runt, so I was an easy target for them.

However, when it came to my sister, I never held back. One day on the playground at recess, my sister came up to me and told me that some boys in her class pinched her on the butt and chest; she was only in the fourth grade. I ran over to the side of the school where all the fourth graders hung out and started screaming and yelling at all the boys in the fourth grade class. I made them all line up against the wall and started yelling at them trying to get the ones who did it to confess. No one would say anything. So, I shouted, "I am going to kick all your fucking asses and beat the living shit out of all of you unless someone tells me who pinched my sister." After that, their fellow classmates ratted out the three who did it. I dismissed the rest of them and kept those three boys against the wall. I told them that if I even caught them close to my sister again, I would kill them. They took off running.

A week later the principal came down to my sixth grade class and pulled my teacher and I out of class. She told me that three boys from the fourth grade had been coming down to her office for a week and calling there mothers to come pick them up from school because they are afraid I was going to kill them. I explained to her what happened and she told me that she might have to expel me. I told her that I could have my dad come down to the school to talk to her. My teacher told the principal, "I don't think you want his dad down here!" When she left he told me that he was on my side and not to worry.

I finally made it to junior high, the year was 1982 and I was twelve years old. However, it turned out that it would be the worst two years of my life. At the end of the seventh grade my mom and step-dad had moved to Arizona to be with my mother's parents and brothers. My sister and I were to move to Arizona after I finished the eighth grade. Meanwhile, I got picked on and teased more and more. I became the brunt of everyone's jokes. I played football, but I was so scared of all the other bullies on the team that I did not play very well. I used to get the hell beat out of me every day. I remember my dad coming to my football games. I remember seeing the disappointment on his face at my poor performances. I always felt bad that I had let my dad down. My dad was a great football player. I remember him telling me about how he played with a broken collarbone and how his helmet did not have a facemask. I remember all of his stories of toughness and I remember how I was weak and timid, scared of everything, even him.

The first period of the day was gym class. There were three guys who would beat the daylights out of me. Two of them would hold me down while one of them punched and kicked me and then they would switch. When I went to the next class these same kids would come up to me and raise their fist like they were going to hit me and I would wince waiting for the blow. They would yell, "flinch" and punch me as hard as they could in the arm. I would come home with black and blue arms and a cut up face.

My dad would not get home from work until six o'clock in the evening. I got home from school at approximately two-thirty in the afternoon. I would have to call him and let him know I made it home. The school was down the street from our house. When I would call him he would ask me, "So did you get beat up again today?" My answer was, inevitably, "yes". He would yell at me for not fighting back. So, not only was I scared to death to go to school, but I was also scared to come home. There was nothing I could do. I had to just take it.

One day my dad finally told me that if I did not fight back he would not let me back into the house until I did. So, the next day I went to school trying to figure a way out of my situation. I got to gym class and we were playing a basketball game where you would shoot the ball and whoever got the rebound would shoot next. Well, I got the rebound and one of the kids ripped the ball out of my arms. I had become so overtaken with rage that I did not even think and I pushed him. He said, "Oh, you want to fight, eh!" I thought to myself, "what are you doing idiot, you'll get your ass kicked." I went through with it anyway because of what my dad had told me the night before. I swung and when I did that, he connected with a punch right in my mouth. I blacked out. I regained consciousness on the gym floor, in a pool of blood and a hole in my lip, which my lower teeth were protruding through. The gym teacher did not say anything to the kid. He just mopped up the blood. I stayed in school all day with that hole in my lip and of course everyone teased me about that for the rest of the day.

At this time in my life the anger and rage inside of me was building. It started to become an emotion that overtook all of my other emotions. Anger kicked all the other emotions out of my body and I was left with pain. It became my driving force in life. It was the only thing that got me through everyday. One day, I even got angry with my father. He was screaming at me for something I had done wrong, again. I became enraged and I put up my fists to fight, just like he was always yelling at me to do. He then said, "Oh you want to fight eh?" He then punched me square in the chest and knocked me down on the floor. I had lost my breath and he began to kick me. He finally stopped and told me never to raise my hand to my father again.

I finally had become so fed up with living every day in fear I was ready to do anything. One afternoon, as a few guys were chasing me home from school, I came up with a great idea for the next day. I could run very fast being that I was so skinny. I got into the house and before my dad got home I took out a left over M-80 I had from the fourth of July, which I kept in the garage, and painted it with rubber cement. Then, I dipped it into a box of BB's, most of them fell off but some remained. I took it to school with me the next day and kept it in my locker.

As I left school that day I put the M-80 into my jacket pocket and started walking home. As usual, I was chased home again. I took out the M-80 and lit it on fire. I turned around and whipped it as hard as I could in their direction. Then I ran like hell through the neighbors' front yards, in between bushes and trees, trying to avoid getting hit myself. BAM! I heard it blow up and I dove onto the grass in a neighbor's front yard. Then I heard screaming and yelling and I got up and ran home yelling, "Don't fuck with me again assholes, or next time it will be worse!"

A Line In the Sand

The summer of 1984 arrived and my sister and I moved to Arizona. I was glad about having an opportunity for a new start and yet petrified at the same time. I worried, "What if the kids here were just like they were back in Detroit?" As far as getting picked on, things were better in Arizona.

I really got into weight lifting. I was tired of being smaller than everyone else. I used to work out three hours every day, eat healthy and take all kinds of vitamins. My friend Jerry and I, whom I met in ninth grade, lifted weights together. We used to weigh ourselves to see how much weight we had gained. We would completely stuff ourselves with food. And a couple of times a week would go to a local hamburger joint in town and get giant milkshakes.

I also liked to run track. I trained hard. There were days I would run until I was so weak and ready to pass out, that I would lay on the track field for an hour after everyone had gone in and showered up. I would get back into the locker room and no one would be there except me. I would give one hundred and ten percent to be better than everyone else. By this point in my life I was bound and determined to be someone. I was tired of getting picked on and getting treated like my life was worthless.

I ran the one hundred-yard dash and the long jump. I would run very hard, so hard in fact, that one time I fell forward onto my face and arms on the track when I crossed the finish line. I shredded my elbows. For a week they bled and leaked fluid until they healed. I always got beat in the one hundred-yard dash, but I never gave up. My best long jump was sixteen feet.

I made a lot of friends, both boys and girls. I never had one particular girlfriend when I was in high school. I was friends with a lot of girls. I figured why ruin a good thing. The school I went to was a school that was mostly made up of kids from very wealthy parents. However, my parents were not rich by any means, but we did okay. I drove a 1950 Chevy pick-up truck to school, which my step-dad bought me for eight hundred dollars. The truck burned six quarts of oil a week and it still had the original engine. My government teacher even chewed me out one day because he got stuck behind me in traffic and had to breath the blue cloud of smoke my truck spewed. He told me to get it fixed and I told him to give me the money and I would. I used to spend a lot of time working on that old truck. I tinkered with the engine and replaced the brakes, windows, etc. My mom used to tease me and say she could hear my truck coming from a mile away because of the cherry bomb muffler I had on it. I put Mickey Thompson slicks (wide tires) on the back end of the truck. I also had the rear end lifted so the truck was at an angle, sloping down towards the front end.

Most of the other kids at the high school I went to drove fancy cars. One year I asked a girl named Patrice to the homecoming dance. She drove a Mercedes Benz convertible to school. The first thing out of her mouth was, "What kind of car do you drive?" I got mad and said, "You're going to fuck me not the truck!" That pretty much ended that relationship.

During the summers I would go back to Michigan to be with my dad. He bought a cottage on Lake St. Claire. We spent our weekends fixing the place up, drinking beer and fishing. We used to catch tons of fish. A lot of times, I would go up during the week by myself and do nothing but catch and eat fish. I would stay there until my dad and sister would come up on the weekends. I enjoyed spending time alone. My sister only stayed in Arizona one year and moved back to Michigan. I ended up staying in Arizona.

My dad would get laid-off a lot in the summer. He worked as a mechanical engineer for the auto industry. So that gave us a lot of time to fix up the cottage and fish. I once caught a Muskie that was forty-one and a half inches long and weighed twenty pounds. It took me forty-five minutes to get it in the boat. I also learned to filet Walleye in six seconds. Michigan had not changed much since I left.

One day, I was in front of my house walking home from my friend Derek's house, with our other friend Lonnie. We were going back to my house to get a stash of beer we had and bring it back to Derek's for his birthday. While in front of my house these three kids in a Chevrolet IROC car, who were in the local Albanian gang, pulled over and mugged us with a Saturday Night Special pistol. I was extremely enraged by the whole moronic event, but I knew that was not the time to do anything about it. I did not want to get shot.

Several weeks passed by and I was painting the house for my dad and I heard my sister and her friend Darlene screaming in front of the house. I walked over to where they were and there were some Albanian guys picking on them. Low and behold it was the same guys who mugged me earlier. I hopped the fence and asked them "If they had a fucking problem" and they replied by pulling switchblades and chasing me. So I ran across the street where five guys were doing landscaping. I yelled to them for help. They all grabbed shovels and gave me one. We said, "Come on mother fuckers lets dance!" Needless to say the Albanian kids had decided it was time for them to leave and rightly so. We would have kicked the hell out of them.

However, I was not done with them. I wanted to teach them a lesson, but I waited for the right time to strike. Later that day I was on top of the ladder painting the house. I happened to look over to the school where the Albanians had been hanging out. They were going home. One went the opposite way and the other two were coming back towards me. So I climbed down from the ladder and went into the garage and got a crescent wrench. I then went into the neighbor's yard, which had a wooden fence along the sidewalk. Our fence was chain link and they would have seen me. However, the neighbor's fence was just short enough to hop over and had slits in it, which I could peak through without being spotted.

When they got close to me I jumped over the fence and grabbed one of them by the shirt and cracked him in the arm with the crescent wrench. He went down and his buddy took off running and left him lying there. As he ran away I said, "Tell all your stupid fucking Albanian boys not to fuck with me again or I'll kick the shit out of all you assholes!" I then went into the house. In the mean time the other guy got up and went home. I never had a problem with them again. My dad found out what happened and started yelling and screaming at me because he thought they would come back and burn the house down.

My dad is six feet tall and at this time he weighed about two hundred and twenty pounds and was built pretty well. I always remember his legs. They were huge like tree trunks. He always lectured me about how it was when he was in the Army in 1957 freezing to death in Germany, while out on training exercises. I always thought that he would have been the perfect drill instructor.

Dad was a hard man. I had mentioned earlier, someone once told me you pick your parents before you come into this world. I must have picked my father, as well as I had chosen my mother. From my mother I received the sensitive caring side of me and from my father I received toughness. It is a skill that would enable me to make it through life. It now seems to me that he knew what lay ahead of me and he prepped me for it. To this day, I rely on this skill called toughness. It has served me well. However, one must be careful with toughness. There is a fine line between being tough and being stupid. You must not cross this line. This, I had to figure out on my own.

My dad once told me that he was much harder on me than on my sister because some day she would grow up and get married and have a husband who would take care of her. I on the other hand, would grow up and move out of the house and I would be on my own and some day I would get married and have a family of my own to take care of. No one would take care of me. He said the world was a rough place and I would have to be tough to survive. This was something I had already figured out by then.

One time I was helping my dad put a depth finder on his boat. He had a boat with a center console, which is where the steering wheel was located. I had to reach under it to put the nuts onto the bolts to secure the depth finder. I could not see under there and I put two nuts on the same bolt. My dad went ballistic, screaming and yelling at the top of his lungs. I said, "Jesus Christ dad, you don't have to yell. All I have to do is take it off."

"What the hell are you going to do when you get into the Marines? They're not going to sweet talk you. They will yell at you worse than me and beat the shit out of you."

"I expect that out of them dad, not out of you." My cousin and the neighbors used to say that boot camp would be nothing for me after living with my old man. They said, "Those drill instructors wouldn't have shit on him."

He yelled so loud that our neighbor eight doors down came down to check on me and see if I was all right. By this time in my life, I was so fed up with everything that I had to get away.

School Days

By this time, I already knew I would join the Marine Corps. It was something I felt I had to do. I used to confide in my grandfather a lot. I would always ask him what to do when I was in trouble. I remember spending a lot of time with my grandparents. I always wanted to go spend the night at their house, even when I was a teenager. I used to love to go to the library with my grandpa. We would come back home and the both of us would stay up until one o'clock in the morning reading. He read and I mostly stared at him. I was amazed at how fast he could read.

My grandpa was a very smart man. He was the smartest man I have ever met. You could ask him a question about anything and he had an answer. He never went to college. He just worked hard all of his life and raised a great family. He always tried to teach me lessons. I remember one time my friend Derek and I wanted to start our own movie theater in Derek's garage when we were ten. We borrowed my dad's movie projector, but it had no light bulb. So my grandfather, who worked for Bell and Howell, told me to type up an invoice and he would deliver the light bulb. So Derek and I did just that. Grandpa delivered the light bulb with a bill for ten dollars. Derek and I were shocked. I told grandpa I did not have ten dollars. Grandpa said, "No money, no light bulb. Welcome to the business world." So, Derek and I sold some of our baseball cards and bought the light bulb.

I still remember the day I was over at my grandfather's house and asked him what I should do with my life. He said, "Join the Marines, those are the boys." When grandpa told me that, I knew this was the right decision for me. I listened to everything my grandpa told me. I think about those experiences with my grandfather often and I think about how nowadays young people seem to ignore older people. Kids now have futuristic libraries and computers, which seem to have replaced older people. It is a shame. My grandfather was a plethora of knowledge and experience. He taught me a great deal. The lessons he taught me could never be learned from a book or a computer.

So, when I was in eleventh grade, in 1986, I ran away from home in Arizona with two friends. I hung around with three guys Jerry, Randy, and Larry. My parents did not like Randy. I was always getting lectured and interrogated every time I hung out with him. I thought to myself, "I finally found some people to hang out with who accepted me just the way I was and they didn't beat the shit out of me on a daily basis. Now my parents are angry at me for having them as friends!"

They were only thinking of my best interests, but you do not see those things when you are a kid. So, Randy and I decided to run away. Larry went too, but only because he was our friend. Randy had a bad family life at home and that is why he decided to run away. Our code name at the police department was the "Red Dawn Boys". We had three shotguns, a 7mm Mauzer rifle, a few pistols and thousands of rounds of ammunition. We were going to live in the woods in British Columbia. We researched everything in the library for six months before our departure. We made it all the way to Seattle, Washington, from Arizona. Larry's uncle, who happened to be the local sheriff, arrested us.

During my high school years the Marines invaded Grenada to free some American medical students that were hostages. I watched it on TV. I told my mother that when I went into the Marines I would go to war. I told her there has been a war every fifteen years and Vietnam ended in 1975 and that the next war would be in 1990. I felt such a strong urge to go into the Marines. I could not resist the feeling. I really felt like a greater force was making me do it, as if it was my destiny.

I remember the day I joined the Marine Corps. I skipped school and had the recruiter pick me up. It was February 10, 1988, just eleven days after my eighteenth birthday. My mom would not sign the papers for me when I was seventeen. I just waited until I was eighteen and did it myself. When I got home that evening my mom was in the kitchen waiting for me.

She said, "You joined didn't you?"

"Yeah, I did."

She slapped me and started to cry. I left for boot camp on October tenth of that same year.

The last day of high school was quickly approaching. Prom was on the horizon. I knew where I was headed and what I was going to be doing for the next four years. I did not go to my senior prom. I thought no one would go with me, especially since I did not drive a Mercedes Benz like most of the kids I went to school with. Plus, I knew I probably would never see any of those people again, so I figured there was no point in going. I had a friend who was a grade behind me. He came over on prom night and we sat in my bedroom listening to records and drinking a twelve pack of beer.

The big day was now only twelve hours away. I was set to leave for boot camp in the morning. I had to be outside at four-thirty, before the sunrise, for the recruiter to pick me up and take me to the Military Entrance Personnel Processing Station (MEPPS). I was so nervous that I hardly slept a wink that night. Here I am leaving my family and friends and when I come back, I would be a different person. I was excited about the challenges that lay ahead of me. I was confident I could make it, after all, it could not be any worse than Detroit!

3

"Morning Has Broken"

> *"Morning has broken like the first morning. Blackbird has spoken like the first bird. Praise for the singing. Praise for the morning. Praise for the screaming fresh from the world."*
>
> By Cat Stevens

I finally made it to the MEPPS. The other recruits and I were herded through like cattle. After the military personnel finished processing all of us, we were segregated into our chosen branches of service. They sent the group of us that were going into the Marine Corps into a room and told us to have a seat. About ten minutes later, a Marine Sergeant strutted into the room. He slammed the door shut and he started screaming like I have never heard a human-being scream before. "Get the fuck up! Get the fuck up! You stand at attention when a Marine walks into the room you scum bag pieces of amphibian shit!"

My knees were quivering so hard they were knocking. I was sure the Sergeant could hear them as he paraded up and down the aisles of chairs, spewing one-liners at the top of his lungs. The Sergeant informed us of our very low status in his world.

After that was over he turned us loose into the hallway to await our bus ride to the airport. I took the opportunity to call my mother one last time. She answered the phone and I said, "mom." She said, "yeah." I just started crying and I could not stop. My mother asked me if I wanted to come home. She told me she would come pick me up that minute, but I told her no. This is something I have to do.

We were finally picked up and driven to the airport. They had us board the plane and before you knew it, we were in the air. We landed in San Diego, California, and were herded again into a staging area in the airport.

Here we all were, from different parts of the country. All of us were on our own for the first time. No one knew anybody. At that moment, I truly felt alone. But, at the same time, I felt like I had a bond with all of these guys. We were all about to go through this together. It is funny, I look back on this day now and realize that this bond I was starting to feel was only foreshadowing the very strong bond I would have with all Marines past, present and future, throughout my life. It is a special bond, a bond that can not be broken. I could run into a Marine on the street and it is as if I have known him for life, like we were long lost brothers who just reunited after years of separation.

People question me about this bond. It is a tough question to answer. I do not think an explanation would give the feeling justice. Marines do not even speak of it to each other, it is just understood. Sometimes it feels as if you are communicating an understanding with each other through your eyes and a handshake and that is all that needs to be done.

I surveyed the staging area we were all standing in and I was surprised at what I saw. There were a few guys who were wearing Marine Corps t-shirts. I thought to myself, "Boy they're in for a world of shit." At that time a thought, which came from an experience I had back in Michigan the summer before I left for boot camp, popped into my head. I was wearing a Marine Corps t-shirt and one of the neighbor's friends came over. He was a Marine in Vietnam. He told me I did not rate to wear that shirt. I thought, "What a prick, who does this guy think he is." Of course my dad told him off and said I was going into the Corps. The guy looked at my dad then me and said, "Yeah, well he didn't make it through boot camp yet!" At this point I was beginning to understand what he had meant.

The next thing you know we were all off to the Marine Corps Recruit Depot, San Diego, California. As we drove through the front gate in our bus, the Marine guard flipped us off. I thought, "I am really going to be a Marine." At that point I became motivated to become a Marine.

The bus arrived at its destination and a drill instructor (DI) that sounded and looked like Darth Vader, got onto the bus and started screaming and yelling in true Marine Corps fashion. "The first and last words out of your mouths will be Sir! Is that understood you assholes?"

"Sir, yes Sir!"

"I can't fucking hear you freaks. Sound off like you've got a pair!"

"Sir, yes Sir!"

Then, he really started screaming. "Get the fuck off of my bus! Get the fuck off of my Marine Corps bus you fucking maggots! There will be no pushing or shoving. If any of you ladies touches me on the way out the door, you will die! Get the fuck moving now or I'll start moving your slimy fucking asses for you!"

At this point I was not even thinking anymore. I was confused and dazed. I just started moving towards the door. I was really ready to soil my pants as I moved towards the bus door, as the DI was standing in it sideways, limiting the amount of space in which we were to exit through.

I looked into his eyes as I passed and I saw a glare like I have never seen before. It was like he was possessed. "What the fuck are you looking at you scroungy fuck. Don't look at me or I'll gouge out your eye balls and scull fuck you to death!" I looked down at the ground immediately and got the hell off of the bus. From that moment on, life was pure hell—again!

I got off the bus and there were several DI's running this way and that screaming and yelling. They all were giving us different directions, and for the recruits, it was a giant monstrosity of utter confusion. One of the DI's got right in my face and pointed to these yellow footprints on the cement. He started yelling at me to get my rear end over there or I would not have a bottom to hang my pants on. I remember his eyes. They looked as if he too was possessed. His eyes were all glassed over and blood shot and the veins were popping out in his neck and on the sides of his head by his temples. I proceeded to get onto the yellow footprints and await my next tongue-lashing.

The next thing they made us do is go get our haircut. They put us in one big line in front of the barbershop on base. They marched us in one at a time. There was a bunch of bar-

"Morning Has Broken"

ber chairs and barbers. In a matter of seconds I was bald. I was amazed at how fast they actually got all of us through there.

That first night they kept us awake all night. We got our uniforms, filled out mounds of paperwork. That next morning they sent us into the chow hall for chow. We were herded through the line. We just put our trays up to the cooks and they slopped food down on them. We sat down at tables and we were told we were not allowed to look up from the tray or talk. If we did, they would assume we were done and they would take our tray and chow would be over for you.

We had about five minutes to eat. I sat down and put all of my food into the middle of the tray. There were now watery powdered eggs, hash browns and toast piled into the center of my tray. I just started shoveling food into my mouth as fast as I could. The next thing you know, I had to throw up and everything came up into my mouth. I kept it closed and looked at the DI. He just looked at me and said, "You'd better swallow it boy!" So, I did.

For the first three weeks of boot camp the drill instructors picked on everyone, screaming, yelling and hitting. They wanted to find out who was mentally and physically week. The ones who were weak got picked on until they had been deemed physically and mentally fit for Marine standards.

During the first week of boot camp you get assigned three DI's. These DI's get everyone checked in, fitted into uniforms, haircuts, shots, and they introduce you to marching in formation.

After we got into our barracks and assigned racks (beds) we had to take a "piss test". We all went into the head and were told to urinate in a little clear cup. Well, there were a few of us who could not process the request. I was one of them. The drill instructor started screaming at me to fill up the cup or he would court marshal me for disobeying a direct order. I tried so hard I thought I was going to rupture a kidney. Eventually, I did please the drill instructor.

That first night we had to take a shower and shave. They crammed about one hundred guys into this tiny shower room. There were several poles with about eight showerheads around them in a circle. They told us we had a minute to shower. I lathered up like a mad man.

Once our minute was up, they herded us over to the sinks to shave. The whole time the DI was screaming and yelling at us. He told us we had a minute to shave. There were ten of us at each sink, all jockeying for position. It must have taken me thirty seconds to find myself in the mirror. I never saw myself completely bald before and we all looked the same.

I shaved as fast as I could. A lot of us were bleeding, as could be expected. We were then sent to our racks so that we could stand our nightly inspection. There was a guy at the rack next to me who was from Georgia. He was bleeding profusely from every part of his entire face and neck. I thought, "Holy shit!"

Just then, the DI stood in front of the kid from Georgia and said, "Holy screaming fucking eagle shit! What did you shave with, a fucking cheese grater?" I felt bad for him. He had to be in pain.

A few days later, the DI sat us all down in the front of the barracks on the floor. The DI then asked each one of us why we wanted to become Marines. The best answer I heard was from this kid whose dad lived in South Vietnam during the Vietnam War. He said he wanted to be a Marine because after seeing what the North Vietnamese did to his dad and knowing what it was like to not have freedom, he vowed to protect people's right to be free and he figured the Marines were the best way to do that. He then cried. It suddenly made me feel very good about what I was doing there.

It took a week to get all of us in uniforms, checked in, shots and the whole nine yards. Once that week is over, you get assigned your real drill instructors. These three men are with you for the next twelve weeks. These men are hard. They are mean. Heaven does not want them and Hell is afraid they will take over. They cannot be killed. They are inhuman and incapable of feeling fear. They eat fear and shit determination. They will make all of us into the same inhuman killing machines that someday may be unleashed on an unsuspecting enemy who will be forced to give his life for his country.

The day finally arrived that we would meet our new drill instructors. We marched over to our new barracks. The drill instructors sat us down in the front of the barracks, which was labeled as "the classroom". To the left was an office (duty hut) that was inside each one of the barracks. All of a sudden the door to it opened and a tall, black drill instructor came walking out over to a small podium they had in the front of the classroom.

You could hardly see his eyes because his hat was low on his brow and he squinted like he was looking into the sun. It made you feel like he was trying to burn a hole in your forehead by looking at you. He stepped up to the podium, and in a gritty voice, started giving us this lecture on how they were going to turn all of us into Marines.

During the lecture, one of the recruits was continuously grunting and breathing heavy. He kept getting louder and louder. The senior drill instructor at the podium looked over to the office and made a motion. Then, a few minutes' later three military policemen showed up, subdued him and we never saw or heard from him again.

As that was ending, the senior drill instructor uttered his last words, "My job is to make you into Marines and I will." I was caught up in the moment thinking about how great it is going to be, to be a Marine. Just then my tranquility abruptly ended. Out of the duty hut came three drill instructors screaming and yelling at the top of their lungs. I think we all simultaneously let loose in our pants. They ran out and started yelling at us to get in front of a rack. We scattered like pool balls just after they have been hit by a fast moving cue ball. The drill instructors were running in all directions, this way and that. They were tipping over racks, tossing mattresses, and throwing footlockers. It was total chaos.

Just then the drill instructors said, "Freeze!" So at the moment I was bent over trying to move a footlocker away from my feet. I froze in this position. After all, he did tell us to freeze. I never heard a thing, then all of a sudden in my ear is a drill instructor yelling, "You freeze at attention freak!" When he said that he simultaneously poked me in both my eyes so I would stand up straight. It worked, but now my knees were knocking uncontrollably, again.

Time passed and one day we were out on the obstacle course. One of the obstacles we were required to negotiate involved running up to a rope, grabbing it and swinging across a ditch filled with water. The sides of the ditch were tall enough that if you hesitated in the least bit, you would crash into the side of the ditch and fall into the water.

It became recruit Bradley's turn to negotiate the obstacle. He was a quiet and shy person about six feet tall with a bit of a potbelly. He ran up to the rope slowly, as if he was afraid, grabbed it and swung across the ditch right into the side of it. He smashed his testicles into the side of the ditch and ended up in the water.

The drill instructor came over and started screaming at him to get the hell out of the water. Bradley was having a hard time as he was reeling in pain. The drill instructor kept pushing him to get up by threatening him. Finally, Bradley who had cracked said, "I don't want to be a Marine!" I thought World War III had started! Drill instructors came from everywhere. They started thrashing recruit Bradley. They retrieved him from the water and took him back to the barracks. When we finally returned, him and all of his things were gone. We never saw Bradley again.

At the end of each training day we had an hour to square away our footlockers, take a shower, write letters home and have our physical and mental inspection before mounting our racks for a short night of sleep. Our footlockers had to have everything we owned in them and it all had its proper spot. Our clothes had to be folded perfectly; boots and brass had to be shined.

One night we had just finished our chores and it was time for the nightly inspection. We had to tie open our footlockers so the drill instructor could view their contents. We stood facing our racks with our backs to the drill instructors. When they approached you, we had to turn around with our hands extended with palms down and head turned to the left. When you did this you had an opportunity to report any physical or mental problems you had at that time. It was generally not a good idea to complain. Once this was done they would say switch and you would turn your head the other way and flip your hands over. They would tell you to pop blisters, clean your ears, etc.

The person that slept in the rack below me, and I, used to tie our footlockers open with a bootlace. We would tie the lids to our rack. One night, without either of us hearing him, our drill instructor snuck up behind me. He put his mouth up to my ear and sadistically whispered in my ear about my footlocker being in disarray. I replied that I had run out of time. This was the wrong answer. He said, "Oh, you ran out of fucking time huh!" With my ear still ringing he grabbed my tied up footlocker with one hand and started twirling in a circle in the middle of the barracks. He then let go. My footlocker went flying, hit the ground and my belongings went everywhere.

He said, "You've got thirty fucking seconds to get that shit picked up and put back in your footlocker the way it belongs or you will pay maggot!" I scurried over there in my underwear and started trying to gather all of my stuff. He started counting, "30, 29, 28, 17, 5, 4, 3, 2, 1. Your done freak! You failed again. You owe me. Get on your face. You will do pushups until you fill this twelve inch by twelve inch floor tile up with sweat. This will help motivate you to be a little more expedient next time!" He actually made me do this. I was there quite a while until I just collapsed. Then he let me, and everyone else, go to bed.

A few days passed by and I had to go to sickbay to get an immunization. Upon my return I found my fellow recruits marking their inspection dress belts. Seeing as how I missed the instructions on how to do this I asked the recruit who slept in the rack next to me how to accomplish this task. He told me and I followed his instructions.

Upon completing this task, Sergeant Mack had gazed my way. "Holy screaming fucking eagle shit!" He ran over to me and got right in my face.

"I thought I told you to ask someone if you don't know how to do something."

"I did Sir."

"Who did you ask?"
"I asked recruit Danson, Sir."
"Danson, did this freak ask you how to mark his belt."
"Sir, no Sir!"

Danson lied to the drill instructor and got me into big trouble. I wanted to give Danson what he had coming to him. The drill instructor then said, "I see, you're a fucking liar." He grabbed a footlocker, since he was short, and pulled it over in front of me. He then grabbed a coat hanger from someone. He got on top of the footlocker and started yelling at me. While he was doing this he was jabbing me in the eye with the rounded end of the coat hanger. Danson and I had some words after the drill instructor finished with me.

After four weeks, towards the end of our first phase of boot camp, we were out side marching in formation. I had to urinate really bad. When we stopped for a moment I asked permission to speak. Once I was granted permission to speak, I asked permission to make a head call. The drill instructor had me go relieve myself behind a building and then we were on our way. The very next day, in the same spot no less, I had to urinate again. This time the drill instructor denied me permission to make a head call. We started marching again and he never told me I could go. So I had no choice but to wet my pants, which I did. Luckily for me it was warm out and I dried quickly.

A few days later, we were all standing in formation. We all had our heads turned to the side. We were supposed to turn our heads to the front and count off. Apparently, I did not do this correctly. My drill instructor jumped through three rows of people, landed in front of me, and started screaming at me again. While he was yelling at me, he was poking me in the middle of my chest with his index finger as hard as he could. He screamed at me to repeat the action that I so terribly screwed up. So, I turned my head to the side again and he punched me in the mouth and my head swung around. He then yelled, "That's how you do it freak." I fell to the ground. He started yelling again, "Get the fuck up asshole. I did not give you permission to fall down!" I got up. My knees quivered and my mouth bled. I thought I was going to pass out, we continued on.

The one thing that gave me hope and really revived my soul was our Sunday morning activity. We all had to go to church. After all, the Marine Corps motto is Semper Fidelis, always faithful to your God, Country and Corps. Church was an escape from the yelling, screaming and torture, as I affectionately like to call it. It was as if for that hour all my worries and fears were cast away and I could relax and find an inner peace that I never had before.

We finally finished our first phase of boot camp. For the second phase we were to receive our field training. We would spend the next four weeks in the field learning combat tactics, how to fight, shoot all the weapons that we may encounter in our tour of duty and how to carry an enormous pack through anything for days at a time.

About half way through phase two, we camped at the firing range. We were in a flat area on the other side of the road opposite of the live-fire range. It was mid November, close to Thanksgiving, and getting a little chilly for us at night.

We each carried a shelter-half in our packs. When we would bed down for the night each of us would get assigned a partner. You and the partner would button your halves of the shelter-half together to make a tent. It became a two-man tent.

"Morning Has Broken"

One night, in particular, it became very cold for us. We were in the mountains of Camp Pendleton and it went down to about twenty-eight degrees. It was quite windy as well. I remember freezing all night long, even with the sleeping bag.

During the middle of the night, someone screaming had awoken me and everyone else. "Holy screaming fucking eagle shit it's a goddamn motherfucking white tornado!" It was one of our drill instructors. While he was yelling this, he was running through camp ripping down everyone's tent. Now we were really freezing.

The next morning, all of us still dazed, were herded down to the road for morning chow. We all sat down along the road. There were about one hundred of us. We were handed our meals. The drill instructor told everyone who had a packet of coffee to take it out and pass it up to recruit White. White was a hulk of a man. He joined the Army and when he got out, he decided he would rather be a Marine. He was about six foot one and pretty well built. We soon found out the reason why White was getting nearly one hundred packages of coffee. It was because of what he had done the night before. White was cold and he decided to make coffee to warm himself up while the rest of us froze. Hence, he was the reason for the "white tornado" that night.

Once White received his packages of coffee, the drill instructor told him to dump them all in his canteen cup. Then the drill instructor told everyone who had a little bottle of Tabasco sauce in their MRE, to pass it up to White. So we did. Then the drill instructor made White dump all of the Tabasco sauce into his canteen cup. Now, his canteen cup was nearly full. White was then instructed to add some water. Then the drill instructor asked White if he liked

Cajun coffee. White, rather foolishly said, "Sir, yes Sir." The drill instructor said, "Good, drink up asshole." They made White drink the Cajun coffee. Needless to say White had a bad, bad day.

Later that week, once we finished our live fire exercises, we packed our gear for our hump (hike) back to Camp San Onofre. Our trek would entail traversing a ridge called "Bitch Ridge" and it culminated with a hump over "Mt. Mother-Fucker". Both of which were appropriately named.

The sun was setting and evening began to envelop us. Clouds were rolling in as we approached Bitch Ridge. This ridge is three miles of switchbacks that continually ascend their entire length. I remember looking up this ridge thinking, "What the hell did I get myself into." A thought I had quite often, since my arrival in what I was sure was hell.

We all started up the ridge. I thought it would never end. It just kept going up, up and up. I was sweating profusely even though it was November. My legs were burning. It literally felt like they were on fire. I could not quit though. The result of that would be more painful than what I was feeling at that moment.

We finally got to the top of Bitch Ridge. I thought I was out of the woods now. However, our D.I. blessed us with great news. "Alright ladies get your shit together and get some water. We are going to climb that mountain. The mountain's name is Mount Mother Fucker." I thought, "You've got to be shitting me." The mountain went straight up to the sky. The night had finally engulfed us at that point. We had been humping all day. Now we had to climb this mountain from hell to get home.

As soon as we started our ascent up Mt. Mother Fucker, it started pouring rain of course. The path we were climbing became very slick and muddy. The mountain was so steep that you nearly had to climb up it on your hands and knees. Since it was so slick, I decided to scoot over to where the grass was, next to the path we were on.

I was climbing up the hill on my hands and knees, using the grass for traction. The DI's were running up and down the hill screaming and yelling at everyone. I was nearly to the top. I was the third one up. Then all of sudden my DI grabbed me by my pack and tossed my beaten soul back down the mountain. Apparently he was upset because I was in the grass and not in the mud like everyone else.

I slid all the way back down the hill. Now my rifle and I were completely covered in mud. I was so pissed. I started climbing up the hill in the mud again, using my rifle as a wedge to get some traction, as the rain continued to impede my progress. I finally got to the top and we all went down the other side of the mountain and into our barracks. The next day was Thanksgiving. We were up until two a.m. cleaning our rifles, gear and ourselves.

The third phase of boot camp finally arrived. We were set to graduate on December 23, 1988. The next four weeks would be more physical training, rifle drills, marching and receiving our dress uniforms in preparation for graduation. We also started going back to church again, which was something that I really looked forward to. I swear there were times I thought I was going to lose it, but every Sunday in church, I found the will to keep on pushing it.

I was starting to feel like a Marine. I was close to graduation. I really started to feel strong and confident, like they were really making me into part of the finest fighting force the world would ever know.

One day, we were in the barracks doing our rifle drills over and over again. My bad luck did me in again. I placed my rifle on my right shoulder instead of the left shoulder where it is supposed to go when the DI says, "Left shoulder, arms!" The DI ran over to me and started screaming in my ear.

"What the fuck are you doing freak?"

"Sir, being stupid sir!"

The DI stopped yelling for a second and I thought I had really done it this time. I was waiting to get beaten. Then the DI said, "Well, at least your honest!" I did it. I stumped the DI. What it really was is that I had matured. I made a mistake and admitted to it and accepted responsibility for my actions. That was precisely what the DI wanted me to say.

Two weeks before graduation, we got to call home again and let our parents know we were alive and well. However, all I could do was cry when I heard my mom's voice. Just about everyone there did the same thing. We all bonded together and comforted each other. We told each other we only had two weeks and we were going to make it. The DI's did not say a word. They just left us alone.

About a week before graduation, we were all sitting in the barracks classroom. The DI says, "Hey, Binger. You're from Texas aren't you?"

"Sir, yes Sir."

"Well, there are only two things that come from Texas, steers and queers. Are you a queer Binger?"

"Sir, no Sir!"

"Get on your hands and knees Binger. Miles!"

"Sir, yes Sir!"

"Get on your feet and show us how you fuck steers!"

"Sir?"

Everyone just busted up laughing, including the DI. He cut us some slack since this was the last week of boot camp.

It was finally the night before graduation. The excitement was mounting. The DI brought in a T.V. and a video. We watched a movie called, "Gung Ho". It was a Marine movie of course. All of our parents were eating dinner with the DI's.

We stayed up all night. No one could sleep. The next morning the Senior DI held reveille (a song that is played to wake everyone up in the morning). The first thing out of his mouth at four-thirty a.m. was,

"Serocki, get your fucking ass over here now!"

"Sir, yes Sir! Sir, recruit Serocki reporting as ordered Sir!"

"What's this shit I hear about one of my DI's poking you in the eye with a coat hanger?" "Sir?"

"Last night your mother told me you wrote home and told her this."

"Sir, no Sir."

"Are you calling your mother a liar?"

"Sir, yes Sir!"

"You'd better straighten this shit out at graduation, do you understand me?"

"Sir, yes Sir!"

All I could think of was the tongue lashing my mom was going to get for getting me in trouble on graduation day.

During the thirteen weeks of hell, I was deprived of sleep, perpetually hungry, run to the point of exhaustion and beaten into being a Marine. I was punched in the mouth, poked in the eye with a coat hanger and fingers, screamed at, belittled and built back up into part of the finest fighting force mankind has ever seen.

Towards the end of boot camp, we were all in a huge classroom. There were about one thousand of us. The DI started out by saying, "One out of every four of you will see combat at least once before your first four year tour is up!" I thought, "Yeah right, I will never have to go to war."

Graduation finally came. We were dressed to the hilt. Everything was perfect. We had an indoor ceremony and then marched outside in formation. We stopped in front of the Commanding General and the crowd. The General spoke to us. I will never forget what he said at the end of his speech. "Congratulations, you are now Marines. Everywhere you go, every Marine past, present and future is now your brother. Just remember one thing, just because you are now a Marine do not think you can take over the world. However, as a team, the rest of the world can just stand the fuck by!" I was so motivated and excited at that point I thought my chest was going to burst out of my uniform.

We threw our hats in the air and it was final. We were officially Marines. My parents ran out on the parade deck and found me. My mom, dad, step-dad, grandma and grandpa were there to greet me. The first thing I did was to start to chew out my mom for getting me into trouble. I then found out it was my dad who had told my DI about the coat hanger incident and I had to apologize to my mother and then yell at my dad.

I gave them a tour of the base and we came across some new recruits and my parents got to see them get chewed out. I was glad that was over for me. We decided to go and get lunch. We were all famished. We went to a Mexican restaurant in Old Town, San Diego.

I will never forget that lunch. We all sat down. We ordered. The food finally came. They gave me my plate first and by the time the waitress delivered everyone's meal and drinks I was done with my food and drink and sitting at attention. They all were staring at me in awe. They all were astonished that a human being could inhale food and drink that fast.

That day was one of the proudest days of my life. I will never forget that day as long as I live. I really felt good about setting a goal and accomplishing it. I never gave up no matter how bad it got. This lesson would benefit me well the rest of my life.

I went home on leave for fifteen days, then to my advanced schooling in Camp Lejeune, North Carolina. There I learned how to put in minefields, take them out, place booby traps, disarm them and how to blow every thing that exists into pieces. My occupational specialty was a Combat Engineer. They used to call us "super grunts" because we did everything grunts (infantry men) did, but we had explosives to play with on top of it.

Then I was shipped off to my duty station, Camp Pendleton, California. While I was stationed here we trained endlessly for war. We were always going out to the field for three or four weeks at a time and would come back for a week and then go back out again. All we did was train, train, and train. It seemed like we would spend half the day on physical fitness. We would run five to ten miles a day, lift weights and do the daily seven exercises. I was in the best shape of my life.

While I was serving my tour of duty in the Marine Corps, the action in Panama broke out. I also spent several months on a ship in the Pacific Ocean. Then, about two years into my enlistment the big day finally came when it was my turn.

4

"HEADING OUT TO THE HIGHWAY"

"I've got nothing to lose at all, going to do it my way, take a chance before I fall."
Judas Priest

It was a bright sunny day. The air was fresh and filled with a hint of moisture from the meandering creek below me. I could hear the creek beside me bubbling like boiling water. Klark and I had just returned from morning chow at the local chow hall. It was mid-July and we were at a place called Bridgeport in California, which is a Marine base for mountain warfare training. We were here with our company for four weeks of training. Our training involved humping up mountains whose peaks touched the clouds, then repelling down two hundred and fifty foot cliffs, all while wearing an eighty-pound pack. We also would have one week of survival training in which we would be simulating war and having to fend for ourselves. Two weeks into the training, I had become very ill.

We had stopped for the night on the side of a mountain that was at an elevation of ten thousand feet. The sun had just risen and I felt like death warmed over. In the early morning the Marine who shared my tent with me summoned the corpsman, doc Bill, to come check me out. He was approximately five foot nine inches tall, a little on the chunky side, and like all corpsman, he was in the Navy. He told Sergeant Martin that I needed to get back down to sickbay at once to get medical attention. Sergeant Martin was about six-foot two inches tall and full-blooded Native American. He was as hard as nails and I always looked up to him and respected him. I, however, did not want to leave my unit. What if this was a real war? Mr. "I hate America" (the enemy) would not stop for a break, he would pop me a new blowhole. So I looked to Sergeant Martin for an answer and he shook his head yes, which I knew meant go to the sick bay.

After getting checked out by the Navy doctors I found out I had walking pneumonia. "How the hell did I catch this crap in the middle of summer?" I was pissed because in a week we were to get two and a half days of liberty in Reno, Nevada, and I did not want to miss that.

Klark had also come down with walking pneumonia. The two of us were stuck in base camp while everyone else was out in the field training. Now that Klark and I had eaten chow we had nothing to do until lunchtime. We were on bed rest for a whole week. "Shit, this pneumonia crap sucks, Klark."

"Yeah, it sure does."

Then I said, "I am so damn bored, I wish I could get back on the mountain. I can't take this sitting around crap any longer." While I was whining about having to sit around all day, Klark was foraging through his sea bag for something. All of a sudden he piped up, "Hey, Serocki."

"What", I retorted.

"I have got some Tarot cards, you want me to give you a reading?"

"That shit doesn't work man."

"You'd be surprised."

"Alright, I guess. I could use some good news about now. Besides, it sure beats sitting around here doing nothing!"

Klark delicately opened up a purple velvet cloth, which contained the infamous cards, as if they were priceless crystal vases. "Why the hell do you keep them wrapped up in that cloth like that? They are just fucking cards for crying out loud."

"No they are not, the cloth helps hold in their power. You have to be serious or this will not work."

"Ok, sorry. I will play nice."

"Ok, now think of a question you would like answered. Keep it to yourself though."

"Ok, I am ready."

The question I was thinking of was that I wanted to know what was going to happen to us next. Klark laid the cards out as if he were a Vegas black jack dealer. "Well, what the hell do they say?" The cards were like large playing cards and had pictures of mystical things on them, which meant absolutely nothing to me.

"They say that something bad is going to happen to us, were are not going to like it, but we will make it through it."

"Awe, son of a bitch. We are not going to get to go on liberty now."

"I think it's going to be worse than that", Klark blurted out.

"How could anything be worse than that? We will have been stuck in this hell hole for a month with out a damn beer or one glance at a hot babe."

"I don't know what is going to happen Serocki, I just know something will happen."

The next couple days went by and the rest of our platoon returned from the mountain. Sergeant Martin and the Lieutenant, a young preppie college graduate, with a baby face, discussed my situation and decided to let me go on liberty with everyone else. I looked at Klark and said, "your cards are fucked man, I am going on liberty!"

While in Reno, I had met a girl. I was twenty at the time and very naive as far as women went. However, I fell in love with her and we planned on seeing each other after I completed my training in Bridgeport. She was about five foot six inches tall and had a body any man would kill for. She was beautiful. She had long brown hair. I used to tell everyone she looked like Christina Applegate only with brown hair.

The next two and a half days flew by and the next thing I knew I was back to humping up mountains that touched the sky and repelling back down them. One evening, August 2, 1990, to be exact, upon returning from one of our many training sessions and humps back down to six thousand feet from ten thousand feet, we all were in the large canvas tent we slept in at base camp, preparing to go to chow. The Lieutenant and Sergeant Martin were talking and the Lieutenant looked concerned and serious. They turned around and told us to listen up. The Lieutenant said, "Iraq has invaded Kuwait and it looks like we will be sent over there. We are not one hundred percent sure yet, but the possibilities are high." Next thing I know my hunger pains vanished and all I could think of was what Klarks's Tarot cards had revealed. Could this be the bad thing that was going to happen to us? The Lieutenant then said, "If we do go, it looks like we will be sent to Turkey first and stage everything there. This is hush hush though; so don't run to the phones and call home to tell your parents. We need to keep this a secret. We will know more in a day or two."

Well, naturally, the first thing everyone did, after chow of course, was run to the phones on the base to call home and relay the news. I was confident that they knew we would do this and that is why they said we were going to Turkey. So I got to the phone and called home. My dad answered the phone and the first thing out of his mouth was, "Did you hear that Saddam Hussein invaded Kuwait?"

"Yeah", I said. "We are going somewhere in the next few days."

"Where are you going?"

"I can't tell you dad."

"Your not going over there, are you?"

"All I can tell you is that we are going to a country that is named after what everyone eats for dinner on Thanksgiving."

"You are going to Turkey?"

"You did not hear that from me."

"When are you leaving?"

"I don't know yet. I promise I will call you as soon as I get a chance, but I don't know when that will be."

"Ok son, take care and I love you, I miss you, and I can't wait to see you."

"Me too dad, I have to call mom now."

"Ok, bye son."

"Bye dad."

The next evening we got the news. We were going to Saudi Arabia, not Turkey. Things had escalated to the point where we needed to go there to stop Saddam Hussein from advancing any further. We were told to pack our things and get ready to leave at twenty two hundred hours (ten p.m.). We all piled on chartered busses to head back to Camp Pendleton (southern California), which is where we were stationed. We would not arrive there until six a.m. the next morning.

I could not sleep the whole ride back to Camp Pendleton. I was a little nervous about what was going to happen over the next few weeks or months. I also was excited in a way. I would finally get to see if I could do the job I was trained to do, to see if all this training had paid off. I would finally find out if I was part of the finest fighting force the world has ever seen. The whole time I was contemplating these thoughts, I was listening to a Judas Priest tape I had. I kept listening to one song over and over again, "Heading out to the Highway". It seemed to coincide with the emotions I was feeling and what I was reflecting upon. I was pondering the decision I made to join the Corps and the notion that maybe I had made a mistake. Or, maybe it was not a mistake. Maybe, I would become a hero. Not all the words apply, but most of them do. The song was, in a way, actually motivating me, pumping me up to go, if you will.

> *Well I've said it before and I will say it again*
> *You get nothing for nothing*
> *Accept when you're back seat driving and your hands*
> *ain't on the wheel*
> *It is easy to go along with the crowd...*
> *So, heading out to the highway*
> *I got nothing to lose at all*
> *Gonna do it my way*
> *Take a chance before I fall...*

"Heading Out to the Highway"

*Having a left, having a right
The choice is yours to do as you might
The road is open wide...*

*Where ever you turn, where ever you go
If you get it wrong at least you can know
There is miles and miles of road...*

Judas Priest: Beyond Metal 1977

We arrived at Camp Pendleton around six a.m. the next day. Upon getting off the bus we had to fill out wills, get shots, pack our gear, our rooms, and get issued desert camouflage clothing and gear. That took all day, as one might expect, especially with the military's hurry up and wait policy. After that we were given liberty for the evening. This would be my last liberty, last bit of freedom for God knows how long.

Hart, some other guys and myself went to the mall. I proceeded to buy the biggest knife I could find because I carried a machine gun so I was not issued a bayonet. It made me feel more secure just in case we ever got overrun and had to resort to hand to hand combat. After that we all went to Sizzler Steak House and reeked havoc on their all you can eat salad bar and ordered steak and beer.

I thought to myself, this would be my last real meal. It was all Marine Corps chow from here on out. That probably was also the best tasting beer I ever had. Maybe it was because I knew it was my last for a while, or if I died in combat it would be my last beer forever. It could have just been the fact that I was not twenty-one yet and I still got served. It was a Corona with a piece of lime in it. After dinner we returned back to the base, it was late and we had to get up early to ship out to 29 Palms, California (a Marine Corps base in the desert) to stage everything and get some briefings before we were to ship out.

A Line In the Sand

The next day we loaded everything up and headed to 29 Palms. I was sitting in the passenger seat of a HMMV, which is a wide, low to the ground, indestructible, vehicle that can be converted into different seating arrangements. You can have it set up to hold two in front and a whole squad or equipment in the back, covered or uncovered. You can also set it up to be a four door four passenger vehicle. The top is a soft top, which facilitates these conversions, similar to that of a Jeep.

It was nighttime when we finally left so we would not be as noticeable. However, everyone that passed us by in their vehicles was staring at us with hollow, frightened looks on their faces. There were miles of green military vehicles going down the road like thousands of ants crossing the sand in a perfect column. I am sure everyone knew what was going on. Our deployment had not been on the news yet, but I am sure people expected it.

I remember wondering what the people staring at me were thinking. I saw many faces that night, many concerned looks, and I wondered if I would ever see America again. For a while I felt good, like a hero. I knew I was going to war, but the way those people were looking at me made me feel like a hero. My chest must have been sticking out a mile or so.

That was all interrupted as my rear end felt like it was on fire. It was a design flaw of the HMMV. If you rode in the front seats too long they got very hot from the engine and felt like they were burning your rump like a steak on the grill. I was very uncomfortable, my butt kept sticking to the seat it was sweating so much, and beads of sweat meandered down my face. The ride lasted a few hours, mostly because we were traveling in a convoy and moving slow. I kept complaining about my butt being hotter than hell. Little did I know that very shortly I would be suffering many more uncomfortable moments in the year to come, with this particular discomfort being mild, compared to the rest.

5

WHEEL IN THE SKY

"The wheel in the sky keeps on turning, I don't know where I'll be tomorrow"

Journey

We had been at 29 Palms for almost a week, training in the one hundred and twenty-degree heat of the desert. We practiced infantry tactics, desert survival, how to give IV's, Atropine injections, first-aid to the wounded, and chemical warfare attacks. We practiced a lot of first-aid because there was not enough Navy Corpsman to go around, so when in combat we would have to apply first-aid to our buddies and ourselves if we were wounded.

By this time, I was wondering If we were really going to go or not. I was getting perturbed because I did not want to have to go through all of this and then turn around and go home. After all, we were known as the Desert Rats. That was our specialty. We trained extensively at 29 Palms for desert warfare. Finally, after dark we were told that if we did not get the call to go that night we would go back to Camp Pendleton in the morning and wait there until we were finally called.

Shortly, after everyone had fallen to sleep, we were awoken by shouts of "pack your trash" and "lets go ladies, we are going to war!" This was it, I was going to war. Oh my God, I did not think it was really going to happen. I wanted it to at times, but I never thought that it would actually happen. I was excited in a way because I might come home a hero and I would get to see if I could really do my job.

I put in mine fields, took them out, breached obstacles like concertina wire and booby traps for the grunts and set up demolition charges, all while under fire. They attach engineers to infantry units. They call us super grunts because we do and carry everything the grunts do, but we also perform our other duties and our packs were a lot heavier. We give the grunts a warm fuzzy feeling in their stomachs, as one of them once put it to me, because we get them out of jams they really do not want to have to deal with. They have enough to worry about as it is. Do not get me wrong, grunts are good guys, they can take anything.

At the same time however, I was scared out of my mind. I had no idea what to expect or what was going to happen to me over the next several months. I had no idea how long this was going to take or when I would come home. What was waiting there for me when I got there? I was soon to learn that this would be the routine from here on out.

We were all packed on to buses like sardines. They were like school buses. It was hot and sticky. A few people became carsick. There were so many of us crammed on the buses it seemed like there was no air movement even with the windows down. We rode like this for what seemed like a couple of hours, all the way to Norton Air Force base. Some of us were standing the whole time. From here we were to catch a C-41 transport plane to Saudi Arabia. When we arrived we all piled out of the buses through the door and emergency exit and awaited our next orders in the terminal.

We waited in the terminal for what seemed like an eternity for our flight off the land of the big PX (USA) to Saudi Arabia. To pass the time, I made phone calls home to my dad and then one to my mother. They both asked if I was scared and I replied that I was not. I do not think at that time the possible consequences of the course of future events had set in yet. After that, a few of us went to the barbershop on Norton Air force base and got fresh high and tight haircuts. Then we went back to the hanger and slept some, knowing we were not going to get too much sleep where we were going.

Marines were strewn about the terminal. Some Marines were sleeping on baggage carriers, in trashcans, on the floors, and on their sea bags. It looked as if a magician had come into the hanger and put a sleeping spell on everyone and they fell down asleep right where they were standing. A few people, however, were nervously pacing back and forth.

We finally got on a C-141 headed for Spain. We were told it would be a fifteen-hour flight and it was. We sat on cargo netting benches along the sides of the plane. All our supplies, food, ammo, and the likes were stacked in the middle of the plane. When we arrived in Spain we got off the plane and went into a hanger and had to wait again, this time it was only for a couple of hours. Boredom was already setting in. Most of us just played cards, smoked cigarettes, and talked about what could possibly happen to us.

We finally boarded our plane. This time we were headed straight for Saudi Arabia and this leg of the flight, we were told, would last seven hours. Tension rose and nerves tensed as we rolled down the runway. Then, all of a sudden we heard a loud noise, which sounded like an explosion. Everybody's eyes about popped out of their heads and we thought the plane had been booby-trapped or highjacked. The plane came to a halt. I gripped my machine gun so hard I think I put permanent fingerprints on it.

The pilot came out of the cabin and told us to disembark the plane. We had blown a tire. That was a relief. My heart was beating ninety miles an hour and sweat was rolling down my face. I thought to myself "Is this what its going to be like?" We spent the next day and a half sleeping in a hanger at an air force base in Spain.

We decided to go and get chow. Marine chow is not the greatest in the world. I used to joke that the Marine cookbook was three hundred and twenty seven pages long and all it said was, "just add water!" There are three things I will never eat again the rest of my life, liver, corned beef hash, and chili beans over rice. It seemed like every time we went to chow it was one of those three things. You did not have a choice. You just lifted your tray up and the cooks slopped the meal of the day down on it. To this day I have trouble when people ask me what I want for dinner. I just say, "I don't care just cook something and I'll eat it."

The breakfasts the Marines served smelled like real eggs and even looked better than real eggs. A lot of times the eggs were so yellow they appeared to have a neon green sheen to them. Every time I ate breakfast I used to think of my favorite book as a kid. It was Dr Seuss' Green Eggs and Ham. I thought it would be cool to eat green eggs when I was a kid, but now I felt quite the opposite. They tasted like old shoe leather. Anybody who has eaten powdered eggs knows what I am talking about.

In the Marines, is where I gained my affinity for hot sauce and plenty of it. My dad always would yell at me at breakfast when I was home on leave because I would mix everything in a big pile with the eggs and cover it with Tabasco sauce. It killed the taste of any bad food and also deadened my taste buds so I would not have to taste anything that slipped through the sauce. After years of eating like that it had become a habit and I added hot sauce to everything whether the food was good or not.

We went to the Air Force chow hall and got in line. When I got to the lady who was serving chow I held my plate up and she said,

"What would you like?"

I said, "I want chow."

I thought she was trying to be funny. After all, what else would I be doing in the chow line? She repeated her question and pointed to the three different meal choices. I said, "Holy shit, you mean we get a choice."

"Yeah you always get a choice. Where are you guys from?"

"We're Marines from Camp Pendleton, California."

"Oh," she said. "That explains it."

"We usually don't get a choice. We eat whatever they put on the plate. And believe me, it ain't that good."

We all went and sat down at a real table, round, with four chairs. Not like the picnic tables and benches we had in our mess hall back in the real world.

After we ate, much to my and everyone else's amazement, someone came and cleaned our table for us and took our trays. The chow was outstanding. We all decided that this was the place to be. This was definitely high-class living. We passed the rest of the time by playing cards, sleeping, and being interviewed by Airforce journalists. They asked questions like "What's the worst part about all of this?" Or "Are you scared?" All we could talk about was the awesome chow we just had and that the worst part so far was the boredom.

We were finally able to get back on the plane heading to Saudi Arabia. As I mentioned before, I carried a machine gun. It was an M60E3. It shoots about two hundred 7.62mm rounds a minute and weighs approximately twenty pounds. I was only given two hundred rounds and we were told that when we landed we were to expect to be attacked as we got off the plane. So we had to be prepared. I thought to myself, "There better not be too many of them, I only have two hundred rounds!"

6

HOTEL CALIFORNIA

> *"We are all just prisoners here of our own device and in the masters chambers, they gathered for the feast. They stab it with their steely knives, but they just can't kill the beast. Last thing I remember, I was running for the door. I had to find the passage back to the place I was before. Relax said the night-man; we are programmed to relieve. You can check out anytime you like, but you can never leave."*
>
> Words and music written by Don Felder,
> Don Henley and Glen Frey

We finally landed at a Saudi Arabian airport. We came to a halt, my heart was pounding, my breath heavy, and I was sweating profusely. The young airman opened the door and we started piling out of the plane ready for what ever was going to happen next. I remember seeing the sunlight shining through the door the airman had opened. It was like I was entering a portal into another dimension of time. It was dark like a cave inside the plane and light outside. I knew that once I entered that light I would begin a metamorphosis that would change me forever. I could never return to the way things were.

All I could hear was my rapid breathing and my heart pounding. It was as if time stood still. Then as I ran past the airman, time resumed its normal pace and I began to hear other noises. The airman shouted, "Good luck boys, hope to see you on the trip home." Then I ran out into the sunlight. I got onto the tarmac (flight deck) and ran to my position and hit the ground and rolled, ready to spray lead down range and waiting for bullets to zing by my head.

We trained to deploy various formations for different situations. When we disembarked aircraft, we were to spread out around it in a circle. I was glad I was off the plane. I waited for gunshots, explosions, or anything, but nothing happened. Then the feeling came back to my body. The black tarmac was hot. I felt like an egg on a sidewalk in an Arizona summer. It was one hundred and thirty degrees outside. Heat waves radiated off the ground. The air was thick with the smell of diesel fuel and asphalt. My nose burned as I was inhaling the noxious fumes. When I had peered out to the horizon, the silhouette of the desert that lurked out beyond the rows of barbed wire was blurry from the heat waves radiating off the flight deck. I kept my eyes glued on the perimeter. Sweat ran into my eyes, burning them causing me to squint even more than I already was. It was so hot I thought they would have to peel me off of the ground. I could actually feel my skin burning through my clothes.

By now, everyone had disembarked from the plane and they were situated in their positions. We waited for a few minutes but alas; there was no gunfire and no Iraqis. So far so good I thought, except for the heat. We then got up and maneuvered into the airport terminal building where we waited for quite some time. Some Marines who had been there for a few days, gave us bottled water.

We were sitting on our gear and complaining how hot it was. We all had helmets, flack-jackets, long sleeve shirts, pants, boots, one hundred pound packs and deuce gear with canteens on. All of this stuff made it even hotter. I rolled up my sleeve and was admiring the beads of sweat on my forearm. They were bigger than any bead of sweat I had ever seen before. It looked like I was covered with thousands of water blisters. Within a matter of thirty minutes we all were completely soaked. I said to someone, "It has to be two hundred fucking degrees." He then said, "Yeah, I think we are really in hell this time."

There were other units here unloading supplies from aircrafts and organizing them into rows. There were others out on the perimeter watching the horizon for enemy activity. We did not know what to expect. I had no idea where I was yet. The only thing I was sure of was that I definitely was not in the United States anymore. I saw very few signs of plant life anywhere, only miles and miles of sand. The sun was so bright that day it hurt to open my eyes. You had to constantly squint. Lots of guys had sunglasses, but I wear glasses so I was out of luck.

We remained here for the rest of the night. We slept outside amongst all the supplies and against the wall of the terminal building. I could not sleep that night. Every time a flare went off on the perimeter so did my adrenaline glands. I could literally feel the adrenaline surging through my veins supplying my muscles with get up and go. I did not know if Iraqis, animals, or other Marines set the flares off. I could not calm down enough to sleep.

It did not really cool down much that night. The only difference was that the sun was not beating down on you and practically igniting your clothes on fire. It was also very humid, like being in a jungle. The sun finally came up the next day. I was glad because I could see to the horizon again. I felt like a little kid being scared of the dark. The night was scary here.

We finally loaded onto buses that were like school buses and local Arabic drivers drove them. After riding on the bus for a while I could tell it was getting close to noon because of the sun's position in the sky. The bus was getting very hot and humid. This little bead of sweat started rolling down my back and my eyelids started to flutter and my head fell. I was asleep. Then all of a sudden somebody had started to scream like they were dying or giving birth and I jumped up and said, "What the fuck is that?" My Staff Sergeant said, "Calm down Serocki he is only praying." Everyone else was laughing.

The bus driver had something that resembled a rosary in his hand and he was praying while he was driving, which apparently involves singing like you are in severe pain. Staff Sergeant said it was one o'clock. He then said, "They pray several times a day here. Once very early in the morning, around noon, and again in the evening." I was mad. The first chance I got to sleep and someone woke me up because they had to sing. "Why couldn't he say his prayers silently like I do", I thought to myself. I then said to the Staff Sergeant, "Man, this place is whacked."

We finally arrived at a shipyard on the ocean. We stopped and disembarked the bus in front of a big aircraft hanger. It was called Al Jabayl. This was where we would be staying for a while, but no one knew how long. The hanger was very large, but barely big enough to house all of us. We were packed in like sardines. It got hot inside the hanger. It was like being inside a microwave. It was better than being outside though, where the temperature reached one hundred and thirty degrees and you had to deal with direct sunlight. At least in the hanger there was shade.

We slept on the cement on top of our ponchos and poncho liners. We were given three meals ready to eat (MRE's) a day. We were also given water. There were no showers and we would run a couple of miles around the shipyard every day, with guns in hand of course. I had to carry that M60 machine gun with me, which weighed approximately twenty pounds. Each box of ammunition I had contained one hundred rounds. These boxes of ammo weighed ten pounds each. I carried two boxes of ammunition. As you can imagine, running while carrying nearly forty pounds in extreme heat is not easy. We were Marines though, we were expected to take it.

While we were running, we sang songs about death and killing Saddam. We did this day in and day out. The conditions so far were less than hospitable and we were not treated very well either. In a letter home to my dad and sister I wrote:

August 12, 1990

> I received your letter. It really boosted my moral. Everyone's moral is pretty low after we got our brief on what mustard gas and nerve gas would do to us. I will receive mail so keep writing me. Tell Lonnie too. I may not be able to write all the time but I will when I get a chance. I love you all very much. I'm fighting this war to make a better place for you all to live in and for that flag which I love

with all my heart. There's a lot of blood and sweat in that flag, some of which is mine. I'm very proud of what I am and what I stand for. Not everyone can hold the title I do or feel the pride I feel. But what I can't understand is how all those other guys can party and watch my buddies and maybe me, die so they can still party and still live with themselves. We are the scapegoats of America I guess. Like the old saying goes, you don't know what you've got until it's gone. I guess only a soldier could really understand that saying. I am leaving for the Saudi Arabia border in the morning. They said we could be there from 3 to 6 months living in damn fighting holes. I carry a M-60E3 machine gun. Which is what Rambo had. Ask Al Boroski, he'll tell you about it. It's good because it will keep me out of putting in mine fields. I'll be security. We are going to put in the largest minefield in USMC history. The only bad thing about the M-60 is that I'll be on the front lines with the grunts. The temperature there is 120–130 degrees with 80–100% humidity. We won't have any showers, hot meals, nothing at all. All I have in my pack is chemical warfare gear and water. We got rid of every thing else. They are expecting 50,000 to 100,000 casualties in the first 6 months if they use gas. They said this will be the worst war for U.S. GI's in America's history. I'll try my best to stay alive. Bye, Bye for now.

Love very much,
Robert

In another letter home, to my dad in Michigan and also to my mother in Arizona I wrote:

August 21, 1990

Hi, how are you all doing? Send me some pictures. Tell Lonnie too (my buddy in Michigan). Call him over to read this letter I don't have time to write him. I am not so good. I am so tired, so worn down. So sick. They treat us like scum. I sleep on the dirty ass cement in a hangar in Al Jabayl about one and half hours from Dhahran. We are supposed to get 16 bottles of water a day, we only get 3. I am so dehydrated, so sick from malaria pills. We still have to run and work with no water. You constantly sweat. It is 120–130 degrees with 80 to 100% humidity. Sunday they brought oranges in for every one. The corporals ate all of them but a few. So I went to get one and they all spit on the oranges in the box and said if I want one to take one. God I feel so bad. I don't think I will last a week and a half. They said I will only be here 2 weeks to 6 months. Pray to god please that it is only gonna be 2 weeks. Sometimes I want to cry but I have to keep it bottled up. Sometimes I want to take my 9mm pistol and shoot myself in the head. I am gonna crack up I can't take it. All I eat is crackers and cheese all day. If I eat anymore I throw up. God I am so skinny now. I have earned 4 ribbons/medals so far. God only knows if they will give them to me. Fucking sand niggers can't even fight their own war. My girlfriend is the only thing that keeps me sane. Some times I just want to die just to get out of here. God I am so tired. 1 to 2 hours of sleep a night. No showers. I have got rotten crotch I think. I am one big heat blister. Please help me dad I am so fucked up man I smoke 2 packs of cigarettes a day. They drill death, death, death, in to our heads ever day. Take the enemy's throat out, chew it up, spit it back in his face, and drink his blood. I am such a cold person. I have had to become an animal, a monster, if you will, just to survive. They said we have to become one massive killing machine to win this war. Fucking rag heads. Steph better keep all of them Albanians away from me when I get home because I will kill them and keep killing them until they are all gone. They have turned me into a bloodthirsty killer. God I hate myself. Somebody please help me! Send stamps, envelopes, and paper. Keep packages small. I have got to go throw up now. I will right back later. I hope I make it home SOON!

Love,
Robert
P.S. Write back fast please!

One day a few of us, all extremely fed up with the shower situation, went out looking for some way just to rinse off. We found this small one floor building in the middle of the shipyard. It had several windows in it. We went up to the building and peered into the windows and much to our excitement we saw a sink. So we then broke a small window and sent the skinniest person through the hole, which was me. There was a hose inside. "Wow!" I thought. "What luck." I hooked the hose up to the sink and it was just barely long enough to run it out the window and up around a beam outside so that it was up in the air like a showerhead. I turned on the water faucet and crossed my fingers. "Yeah!" The water was running. We all got in line and lathered up under the hose and took a primitive shower.

While we were all preoccupied with washing ourselves a Russian ship pulled into the harbor. Someone yelled, "Look, there's women on the deck!" We all started shouting at them and waving to them. Picture it, there were a bunch of stark naked Marines screaming and yelling at Russian women. We had a good laugh about that one later. And of course, as soon as we were all semi clean for the first time in about two weeks, our fearless leaders assembled us for P.T. (physical training) and we all went and ran a few miles and got all sweaty and dirty again. I guess they did not want us getting used to being clean. We were outraged.

We remained in the hanger at Al Jabayl for about two weeks. During that time we went through scud alerts, which, thank God, never materialized. We received briefings on the enemy and his capabilities and what we could expect. In doing this, our mission was explained to us. Our mission was to be of a defensive nature. It was simple. We were to stop any further advancement of Saddam's troops south from Kuwait into Saudi Arabia. By the end of the week, we found out that we would be leaving for the desert and the Kuwaiti border in the morning.

I wrote to my family in Michigan:

August 27, 1990

Dear Dad and Steph,
Well, the day has come that I hoped I would never see, combat. Yes dad, they told us today we are going into combat soon. I can't tell you when but It'll be soon. You don't have to worry about your son pops, I'm hard core. Besides by the time we get to those fucking sand sucking rag heads we'll be doing a mop up operation. I can't tell you what we are gonna do, but the Iraqi's are fucked when us and the

Russians get through with them. Dad and Steffy I want you to know that no matter what happens to me I love you both very much. Part of the reason I'm fighting this war is to make a better place for the people back in the world that I care for. Dad make a good life for stuffy. She's matured very much lately and she's getting a good head on her shoulders now. Some of the things I did like stay in Arizona and letting steph move to Detroit and shit like that was because I didn't want steph to go through all the shit I had to. I wanted to move back home and be with my friends too. I knew what it was like for her. I knew if both of us went that it would really hurt mom. I am her older brother I had to watch out for her. I had to suck it up for her. In my eye's that's what I'm on earth for. To protect the ones I love and the weak and less stronger people. Dad I have obtained an honor that no one can beat. I'm a hero, a U.S. Marine (bad motherfucker), fighting for his country and the ones he loves. Like the corps says, "If I die in a combat zone, box me up and send me home. Pin my medals upon my chest and tell my momma I'd done my best. Momma Momma don't you cry, because the Marine Corps motto is to do or die!" This time I come home I may have two to four rows of ribbons. I am so proud of myself. Every time I hear the National Anthem or see the flag I get goose bumps and I start to cry. There is so much that goes into that flag that civilians take for granted because they've never been to combat. It is my belief that this is what the colors on the flag really stand for. The red stands for all the blood American GI's have spilt for our country. The blue stands for all the tears and sweat that is shed. And the white stands for the fog of war. It's the confusion that takes place when you're under fire. When I get back

if they don't give us free leave I'll take leave at Christmas. Well, that's all for now. I love you all very much. Let Lonnie read this letter. I will see you all when I get home. Bye for now. I love you all very much and I'll write you later.
    Lots of love,
    Robert

7

"VOICE OF AMERICA'S SONS"

> *"Tonight someone will pay. Out in the streets hear the voice of America's sons. Well, they're fighting in the jungles and they're fighting in the streets. They aint playing no games man, they're playing for keeps. Hey little Johnnie when they call on you, tell me Johnnie, what are you gonna do? Turn the radio on with every beat of the drum, go out in the streets with the voice of America's sons."*
>
> Music by John Cafferty and The Beaver Brown Band

We finally had made it out to the desert. All anyone could see was miles and miles of wind sculpted hills of sand. The sun glistened off of the silicates and other minerals in the sand, like light hitting crystals. It reminded me of the sun shining on a fresh snowfall back in Michigan.

The sand was just like beach sand. It took forever to walk one hundred yards. It was constantly around one hundred thirty degrees during the day. At night it went down to about ninety degrees or so.

However, the night brought no relief. It was so humid, like the jungle. After sweating all day you would take your wet undershirt off at night in hopes that it would dry by morning. This was not the case. You would end up putting on a wet tee shirt in the morning.

There were no plants anywhere. The only signs of life were less than welcomed species of insects, such as scorpions and red ants. There was a wild camel or two, giant lizards and snakes. The only other thing out here was us, which the insects fed off of. It was as if the insects were bloodthirsty great white sharks and we were bloody hunks of chum just thrown in front of their faces. They ate our flesh vociferously as if they may never get the chance to eat again. In one of my letters home to my father, I describe our less than desirable living conditions and some of our daily routines. The press also had written an article describing what things were like for us.

August 30, 1990, 12:58pm

> Dear Dad,
> Well here's what I do. During the morning we dig fighting holes. In the afternoon we try to sleep but I cant it's to hot, about 120–130 degrees with 80–100% humidity. It's like the Sahara Desert here. Nothing but rolling hills of sand. At 6:15pm we move out to our fighting holes and we have to stay up all night staring out in the desert. I sleep in the sand on top of my shirt. You constantly sweat then the wind blows sand on you and it sticks to you and

you get this nasty rash that itches and gets all pussed up and people are getting rotten crotch and our feet are falling apart. They have no showers for us except when we go to the rear which is for 1 day every week or so. Sometimes longer, sometimes shorter. We are about 80 miles from the border. We're supposed to get attacked September 5th because there will be a full moon and their religion say's they will attack on full moons. So by the time you get this I'll have been through my first fire fight with the ragheads. This is straight up news pops. 1/7 the 7th MEB which has 7,000 troops, are the only combat ready troops out in the desert. They talk all this shit on the news about how great the fucking army is well listen to this: The 82nd and 101st airborne units are still on ships because they are not ready to fight yet. They've been out there 3 weeks now. The only people on the border ready to fight is the 7th MEB which is me. And the Army said they could do anything the corps could. Bullshit we went from Bridgeport to 29Palms and to the Kuwait border in a week and we were ready to fight and the Army still has there heads up their asses. They're a bunch of pussy's. I know this sounds morbid, but you might as well get used to the fact that this could very well happen…. If we do go to combat there's gonna be 7,000 U.S. marines against 1 million rag heads. So if it happens don't count on me coming home alive. What I just told you is the truth about how many troops are ready to fight. I am here I know. I'm so damn dirty and hot. All my clothes are stiff like starch from my sweat. I'm tired as hell. I'm so depressed we are up against un-winnable odds, but I guess that's what Marines are. Fucking bullet catchers. What a crock of shit. Our own country is fucking us. We can't get no grenades, no bazooka rounds. I only have 800 rounds for my machine gun. We're just plain fucked. Our own government don't even give a fuck about us. I've got the word expendable stamped on my forehead I guess. Well, I have to go dad. I love you a lot and I miss you. God I can't wait to come home!

 Love, Robert

Scottsdale Progress, Wednesday, September 5, 1990:
Marines get lost in time amid desert
Neil MacFarquhar
Associated Press Writer

 IN SAUDI ARABIA- The U.S. Marines call their patch of the Saudi Arabian desert "the twilight zone." The sector south of the border with occupied Kuwait is home to venomous scorpions, snakes like carpet vipers and heat that's almost unbearable. The men never know the exact temperature, and perhaps that's a blessing. "We don't know what day, what month, what time it is," said Lance Cpl. Eddie Zazueta, 21, of Los Angeles. "I think maybe I was supposed to get out last year. This is the Twilight Zone."

 Some men have suffered nasty scorpion stings early in the morning as they groped for their toilet kits. A day in the clinic and they are back on the line. The morning "bath" is perfunctory but important; a nearby army unit that skipped it came down with body lice and dysentery, Hixson said.

 Hot showers back at the base come about every 10 days. Breakfast is a banana, apple, orange or an MRE-"meal –ready-to-eat" Frankfurters are the favorite.

At 7a.m. it's 85 degrees. An hour later, it's 97. By noon it's approaching 120 degrees and the heavy guns crawl under camouflage tents until 5p.m. Sleep at midday is impossible because of the heat.

While we were out in the desert, isolated from an entire world, life went on. Events were unfolding, even in the country we were in, completely unknown to us.

Scottsdale Progress, Wednesday, September 5, 1990:
Saddam: Our kids are dying
Associated Press

"The trade embargo on Iraq is depriving the people of food and medicine," Saddam said in a televised statement read by his spokesman.

"The children of Iraq are dying because of a foolish decision taken by certain people, the children of Iraq are dying because they are being deprived of their food and milk and medicine," the statement said.

But Saddam reiterated that his country would defy the boycott, and said Iraq would be victorious.

We were stationed about eighty miles or so south of the border of Kuwait, but exactly where I was never sure. We set up a small defensive perimeter. We built bunkers and fighting holes and trained during the day. There was one mission that we specifically trained for. About forty miles north of our location was a gas station and a convenience store. It had several hotel like rooms on the north side of the property. There were also several large fuel tanks behind the store. We were told that if the Iraqi army ever crossed the border between Saudi Arabia and Kuwait, heading towards us, they would have to refuel their tanks and other motorized vehicles by the time they arrived at this gas station. So in the event that this could possibly happen, our mission would be to destroy the gas station before they got there, thus trapping them in the desert like an elephant stuck in a mud bog.

We set out one day towards this gas station to train for our possible assault on it. When we got there everyone was assigned a mission. Some people would have the job of clearing out the hotel rooms, some would destroy the fuel tanks, and others would clear out the convenience store. My job as the machine-gunner, would have been to kill everything I saw. I was told my position would be behind some gas pumps across from the store. My Sergeant told me that a few other Marines would go into the store and try to get everyone out. We would only give them one chance to come out because we did not have time to screw around. He then told me if they would not come out that I was to kill everything in the store that was breathing; all the civilians, women, children, everything. I said, "aye aye Sergeant Martin."

We would have had no way of knowing if the people who were supposedly going to be in the store at the gas station, could have been be the enemy in disguise, sympathizers with the enemy or what. We could not trust anyone. The Marine Corps always taught us this, "a Marine on duty has no friends". By letting the people run wild it would only have made it harder for our mission to be a success and increase the chances of us dying, if we had to actually go through with the assault. I was not about to die in that hellhole. I knew that I could not hesitate at the moment of truth. I would have had to just pull the trigger. I knew that I would do it if the situation arose and that is what scared me. The thought chilled me to the bone. What was happening to me over here? I would have never dreamed I would have to possibly do something like this. I knew that now, I would never be the same carefree twenty year old kid that I was when I got here. That day changed me forever. Thank God, and I have on more than one occasion, in the weeks that would follow, we never had to complete our planned mission on the gas station. Our plans changed, we moved our position several times, and I had forgotten about the old mission and began to concentrate on our new missions.

At night we manned the fighting holes we lived in and peered into the darkness of the desert looking for the enemy. I had to dig my hole on top of a sand hill. We dug and dug and dug, but the sand kept filling in our hole. So we were left with little less than a small depression. So, Muir (my assistant gunner) and I went over to a supply area where we kept large beams, like railroad ties, for building bunkers. We grabbed six of them and hauled them back to our pitiful hole in the back of a HMMV. We stacked them two tall around our hole, leaving the back open. If we got into a firefight we would have to lay down behind these beams while we returned fire, so we would not get hit with bullets or shrapnel.

One night in particular we were discussing our positions with our assistant squad leader, Corporal Hart. It was still light out, but the sun was setting. I kept saying, "I have a bad feeling something is going to happen tonight guys." No one believed me, but I was absolutely sure. We went to our holes just before dark. I took my shirt off for a little while. Just as I did that the flying red ants came out by the hundreds. They were landing all over me, stinging me. It was driving me insane. You could run your hand through the air and literally catch a handful of them. I was smashing them all over my body. I just had to sit there and take it. I think I invented a few new cuss words that day. Then they stopped, thank God. I figured I had better go make a sit down head call before they came back and found me hanging my butt in the breeze. Also, I wanted to go before it got dark. I had a fear of getting caught in a firefight with my pants down around my ankles. During the day I could see what was going on, at night you could not see very far.

I went down the hill I was on and found a spot to do my business. So I dug a little hole, shoved my e-tool (shovel) in the sand and dropped trou (pants). While I was balancing myself on my e-tool handle I heard several large insects buzz by my right ear. They just came out of nowhere. They flew somewhere behind me. They flew so fast I could not see them. They sounded like little remote control airplanes. So I just went back to my business of relieving myself and all of a sudden I hear this click, click, click in the sand from behind me. "What the fuck is that", I thought. I turned around and saw several beetles marching in formation towards me. They were about the size of golf balls. "What the fuck are those things," I said. I began to get nervous because I had no idea what they were going to do. They looked mean. I continued to watch them as they marched right between my legs, never breaking formation, and jumped in the hole I dug and landed on my excrement. The next thing you know, they were rolling my feces through the desert. "What kind of sick fucking bug is that?" I blurted out.

I hurriedly finished what I was doing and ran back up to my hole and said to Muir, "You won't believe what just happened."

"What?", he said.

"These fucking huge ass beetles buzzed my tower while I was taking a shit and the next thing you know they were rolling my shit through the desert."

"That's fucking disgusting."

"Now I know this country is screwed up, with fucking insects like that!"

Muir was in amazement. I then named our new friends "shit beetles". Then, as if one of these shit beetles heard what I had just called them, it flew by my head again and landed on the sand and was fiercely marching towards me. So I grabbed my e-tool and repeatedly smashed the beetle screaming, "Die Mother- Fucker, die!" Then I stopped and the beetle got back up and started making clicks and squeaks at me. Muir burst into laughter and said, "He's chewing you out Serocki. He's gonna kick your ass!" I said, "I hardly think so." I then smashed him a few more times with my e-tool and he died.

I told my assistant gunner that I would take the first half of the night and he could stand watch the second half. Normally, I would sit on my flack jacket and have my helmet on the ground next to me. My shirt would be hanging on the wall of my bunker. But, tonight was different. I wore my helmet and flack jacket I was so sure something was going to happen.

I was sitting on one of the beams, which formed the front of my hole. My machine gun was next to me. My area of responsibility was a road and a path that meandered in between two sand hills. My mission was to kill anything that entered the area. Our motto was "If it grows, it goes!" Several hours had passed by. It must have been close to midnight. Then all of a sudden, while I was sitting there, pop, pop, pop! I immediately did a back flip over the beam I was sitting on and locked and loaded the machine gun. I started saying, "Come on motherfuckers. I'm gonna fuck your asses up you cocksuckers!"

Someone had shot at us. "I knew it. I knew something

was going to happen tonight." Then there was a small explosion within our perimeter. Bop, bop, bop! We answered back with a fifty-caliber machine gun. I kept looking over my field of fire. I had not fired a shot yet. We were all responsible for our own fields of fire. You had to trust the guys in the holes next to you. You had to assume that they would cover their fields of fire. And if they died, then you had to do double duty. In that situation you would have to cover their fields of fire also.

We were trained to have discipline when in fire fights. I was not going to shoot until I could see someone. I remembered the drill instructors in boot camp yelling "fire discipline!" They would say, "don't fire until you have someone in your field of fire. You do not want to let the enemy know where everyone is and where all of our weapons are located. Sometimes, they will probe you to find out that information."

I did not want to let the enemy know where all of our heavy guns were and where all of our holes were located. Especially since it sounded like they had a small mortar with them, given the explosion I heard. Besides, I had figured they were just a small patrol probing us to find out what we had, where we had it, and how many of us there were. In the Marine Corps we have a saying, "superior thinking will always conquer superior force."

After we opened up on them with the fifty-caliber machine gun we did not hear any more gunfire. I could not see anyone moving out on the perimeter. It was over. I had survived my first firefight in the desert. My adrenaline was sky high. My heart was pounding so hard, I thought it was going to pop out of my chest. It was invigorating. You could smell the burnt gunpowder in the air from the shots fired and all was quiet again. It was eerie though. Now you knew there was something lurking the dark that wished to kill you. Just as the smells of war were whisked away on the night breezes, so was the threat.

We all started checking with each of the holes next us, to see if any one was wounded. Every one was ok. The Sergeant Major then came by our holes to check on us. The Sergeant Major said the first thing he heard was my machine gun being locked and loaded. We assured him we were ready to kick some ass. My friends kept teasing me the next day. Hart kept saying, "After the first gun shots all I heard was Serocki lock and load his machine gun within a matter of seconds. I heard his bolt slam home and him yelling come on mother fuckers!" After this event had taken place I wrote a few letters home to my family, describing what had occurred that day and I told them about the mission we almost had to complete at the aforementioned gas station.

September 4, 1990

Tom (my Step-dad),
You being proud of me means a lot. If Iraq comes into Saudi Arabia my squad has to blow up this gas station. My job since I'm a M-60 machine gunner is to kill every person that moves there. Women, children, everything. War sucks, but I guess they shouldn't have started this war. You play the game you gotta pay the price I guess.

Dear Mom,
Well, last night we got attacked by the PLO (Palestine Liberation Organization). I am alright, nobody got hurt. Them cocksuckers got away though. We couldn't see them. It was too dark.

though. We couldn't see them. It was too dark. Didn't know where to shoot. I just heard bullets whiz by. I have had to many close calls with death in the corps and one of these days I have a feeling I'm gonna get more than grazed. I get mail from everyone. It takes seven to eight days for me to get your mail. I wrote you once a long time ago. I don't know why nobody is getting my mail. I'm in a fighting hole in the desert about 80–85 miles from the Kuwait border. I can't keep low and out of the way and not take chances. I have to many peoples lives depending on mine to worry about my own. That's my job mom, that's part of the contract that's what made our country. Bravery, honor, dignity and a lot of blood and sweat. I'm prepared to do my job to complete my mission even if it means dying. I have to I'm a Marine. Your just gonna have to realize that now. I have the most dangerous job in the world. I'm here to protect you all. Not myself. If I have to I will die for that flag and to make things safe for you guys. This country was made with men like that and they're still needed. I have just as much chance of dying here as I do driving to Taco Bell. The Marine Corps has a saying that we all go by. It goes like this, "If I die in a combat zone box me up and send me home. Pin my medals upon my chest and tell my momma I done my best. Momma Momma don't you cry, because the Marine Corps motto is to do or die." Well, that's all for now. I love you all very much. Send me a carton of cigarettes please. The package has to be 12 ounces or less so I've heard, send stamps, envelopes and paper too please. Bye for now.

 Love,
 Robert

"Voice of America's Sons"

Dear Uncle Dennis and Aunt Sandy,
I received your letter last night. Thank you very much, it made me feel very good. Nothing could get you used to this heat. It's 120 to 130 degrees with 80 to 100% humidity and no damn shade. Just sand everywhere. With herds of camels roaming all over. I live in a fighting hole in the desert about 80–85 miles from the Kuwait border. So I don't see any women. Just camel herders and desert nomads. I hope I come back to the good ol' US of A soon. This place sucks! I'll be looking forward to raising a little hell in Puerto Penasco when I get back. I'm so stressed out, tired, worn down and dirty. I get a shower maybe once every two weeks if I'm lucky. Last night we got attacked by terrorists. I nearly shit my pants. It was the PLO. Nobody got hurt thank God. But it wasn't fun. I've brushed with death too many times in the Marines and I am afraid I'm bound to catch a serious bullet one of these times. My odds keep increasing. Hopefully It won't happen. Well that's it for now. I liked your joke. I'll write next time I get a chance.
Love your nephew,
Robert
P.S. If you can please send me some stamps, paper and envelopes. I'm running out. You can't buy them here in BFE (Bum Fuck Egypt)

I also had received a few letters from home in that time frame. My parents were asking me a lot of questions about what was going on in my world. They were hearing reports on the news and they were just as confused as I was. Neither of us really knew what was actually taking place. They also told me about things that were taking place in their lives back home. At times it helped me feel like I still had some involvement in their lives and the real world. Often, there letters were the only way I received any information about what was occurring in our little standoff in the desert and about what the President was doing to try to end this conflict. I wrote them all back and tried to describe what life was like for me in the Saudi desert. We changed addresses a lot and I frequently wrote my family giving them the new information. It always worried me when this happened, because I would think they were not receiving my mail or that they would send letters to me with the wrong address on them and they would get lost. They also worried that I was not receiving their mail. At times it seemed like that to them, because of the time it took to send and receive mail. Generally, it took anywhere from seven to ten days to receive mail from home. I was also worried about my girlfriend at the time. I thought she would leave me because I was not home with her. I envisioned our plans of us being married getting whisked away like a piece of paper in a windstorm.

September 5, 1990

> Steph:
> I'm doing shitty, how about you? Hope court turns out good for you, you little heathen. Good luck job hunting. Tell Lonnie I said hi. Who's the bimbo that pranks the house? I've wrote 3 letters before this one. You should have gotten them by now. It takes 7 to 8 day's for me to get your mail. I suppose I do look mean. That's my job to be a major asshole to the enemy. Well, get them ribbons. I expect to see them when I get home. Gotta go now.
> Love ya,
> Robert

Dad,

Hell no I ain't sleeping at 2:30 in the morning. I'm awake in my fox hole looking for ragheads. Well dad, don't let the news fool you. We are right up on the front lines too. That is the corps anyways. The Army is still in the rear because there not ready for combat yet. Waaaaah! Them pussy's. All that equipment you talk about is going to the guy's in the rear, we can't get shit. We've got 7,000 combat troops they've got one million. We have 500 tanks, they have 5,000 so you tell me who's fucked. That's good old George Bush fucking his own troops. They said this is just like Vietnam. The Russians and everyone else is advising us not to attack because they said we will get slottered just like Vietnam. Well now you can see why. Nope no women, beer??????? Hell, I can't even get enough water let alone only getting a shower once every two or three weeks. I don't get no liberty. I live in my bunker while these flying red ants drop on you like rain and bite the piss out of you. It stings like a bitch and bleeds all over the place. Well got to go now.

Love you both lots,
Robert

P.S. Send more stamps, paper, envelopes and a carton of Marlboro red cigarettes. Packages have to be 12 ounces or less.

September 9, 1990

Dear Mom,

I received your card today and grandma's package. Here's a new address because the one you got is the Army and Airforce mail so now we got our own address. I'm still getting your mail so don't worry just use this new address.........

You can send packages and stuff through this address. The desert picture on the card is what it looks like here except there's no blades of grass. I know you weren't trying to put me down about getting married but I'm under a lot of stress here and I may say things I don't mean. I guess I just expected a different reaction. I know it was a lot to dump on you at one time but I had no choice I was leaving and I didn't know if I would talk to you for a while. So you joined a support group huh? It's hell for me too I'm always thinking about home and my girlfriend but your lucky in a way you have someone to talk to I have no one. They just say suck it up, be a man about it. So I have to keep all this tension and aggression bottled up inside of me till I get home and then I probably explode once I get a chance to relax. When I get out of this hole we'll get some time off so I'll bring her out for a few days. You'll like her she's a real sweetheart. She just has this problem of not being able to keep her hands off of me. But I don't mind (ha ha). We'll talk about it all when I get home, thanks I'll need your help. That's cool your sending my picture in to the t.v. station. Don't forget to tape it I can't wait to see it. All the people I know will probably shit when they see it. Send stamps, envelopes, paper, and a carton of Marlboro red cigarettes fast that's the only release I have. Tell grandma I got her package and I said thanks. I don't have enough stamps to write her. I love you to. I hope I'm home soon atleast by Xmas. God I can't take this place. I go to chow at 5:30am and then go build bunkers all damn day in the hot ass sun you get all sweaty the sand blows and sticks to you. Then you come back to here at night and sit awake staring into the desert wondering if you'll see the sun come up in the morning. All these things take a tole on your mind so you'll have to bare with me when I get home. They have these flying red ants that drop on you like raindrops at night and sting you. I have scabs all over my body from them damn things. You can't get rid of them you just got to let them bite you. Then you go dig a hole to take a shit you do your thing and before your done these huge ass beetles (we call them shit beetles) pounce on your shit and drag it away. God you can't even shit in peace! I tried to kill one the other night so I wacked it with my e-tool and it stood upon its hind legs and chewed me out in clicks and squeaks. I had to hit the damn thing 4 or 5 times to kill it. There's a song that kind of say's how it feels to be here. Here are some of the lyrics:

"I don't know where I am going, but I sure know where I've been. Hanging on to the promises and songs of yesterday. I aint waisting no more time. Here I go again. Even though I'm searching for the answers I never seem to find what I'm looking for. Oh lord, there's a break in my strength to carry on. Because I know what it means to walk alone and only see my dreams. Here I go again on my own walking down the only road I've ever known like a drifter I was born to walk alone. I'm just another heart waiting for love's sweet charities. I'm gonna hold on for the rest of my days."

Tell Tom and Amanda I said hi and I love them too. I know it's hard to let go but I will always be around so don't worry. I'm glad your glad I have her cause I really like her. I just worry a lot that we're gonna stay here to long and she's gonna give up on me. I know if she's worth it she'll wait. But it happened so many times with my girl friends in Detroit because I lived in Arizona. I'm kind of scared about that. I don't think I could take that on top of all of this shit. But I don't think it'll happen by what she writes in her letters. Here's a song she wrote for me the other day:

I love you and no one else
But you left me by myself
Cold and lonely, oh so lonely
You know I love you so
Love is breezy, like the wind come and go
So take it easy nice and slow

It made me feel good but it also made me feel bad that I couldn't be there with her. But she knows I had no choice to be here or not. I will thank her for keeping me sane. Well, I have got to go know I will write you later.

Love,
Robert

September 10, 1990, 12:31pm

Dear Dad,
You should receive 3 or 4 more letters including this one. Send more stamps and envelopes and paper and Marlboro red cigarettes please! Thanx for the 10 bucks we went to the rear to take showers today so I bought a carton of this shit brand cigarettes cause that's all these camel jockies had. Here is my new address.........With this address you can send packages. They don't have to be exactly 12 ounces but don't make them to big. This is our own Marine Corps address. I'll get your mail if you

sent it through the other address, just use this one for now on. Well the rest of the men are in the rear. We're the ones on the border in the desert busting our asses. They get showers and air conditioning everyday. If we get a chance to use the PX in the rear which is barely ever, there is nothing left cause them fuckers in the rear buy it all. So they don't have to really suffer with the heat, the bugs, the head games, the dirt, and the terrorists taking pot shot's at you. Well I build bunkers by day and stay up all night in a fighting hole staring at the border. I only get about 2 to 3 hours of sleep a night so I am kind of like a zombie it's a bitch! You can't demand more water we only get what is left over from them cocksuckers in the rear which isn't much. Well they're doing a good job at making me mad as hell. The hanger I was in a long time ago had no air circulation and was hot and humid as hell. Now I just live in a hole in the sand. I'm trying to get through this the best I can. I used to pray but I stopped my prayers were never answered. Things just got worse. I just don't give a shit no more. I just don't care. It's kind of like being blind, deaf, and unable to speak. I don't hear what's going on, I can't see the light at the end of the tunnel and I cant speak, I have nothing to say. I have no emotions no more except hatred and despair. I don't say much any more my face is just blank. Hell there's nothing to say it doesn't pay to talk. I live day by day. Hoping some day to come home. People have shot themselves in the legs and feet just to get to go home by way of the brig it's so bad here. It's gonna take time for me to adjust to home when I get there it's gonna be worse than the last time I was home by far. Dad I don't know who I am anymore. I don't like what I've become. What am I doing here? I see no civilians no nothing it's like I'm not in the world no more. Am I going crazy? God I hope not. Why do I have to stay here and suffer dad? I'm not part of this it ain't my war. It sucks not knowing what's going on, what's happening or if I will see the sun rise tomorrow or not. Dad I'm trying to be as strong as possible but it's very hard. I weaken every day as I take the blows they throw my way day in and day out. I will come home but I'm not sure what kind of shape I'll be in. Thanks for the picture it was nice. Dad no matter what happens to me you have to hang in there and carry on I know it'll be hard but you have to be strong for every one else. Just as I have to be strong and not show all these boots (new guys) that I am hurting inside. But I'm positive I will return home alive. Mentally I may be fucked but that will go away after a while hopefully. All I ask is that I can come home but I get no answer. I am sick of living in the fucking dirt like an insect. What really kills me is fuck face Bush is on vacation during all of this and I'm out here drifting away from reality cause he doesn't give a fuck about us. How could they have the right to play with my life like a little girl play's with Barbie dolls while they watch me suffer on T.V. and go "gee that's too bad, them poor boys." Well fuck them. Well I have to go now dad. Write back soon and send me those things I asked for.

    Love,
    Robert

When I got to Saudi Arabia, I began to pray to God again, just like I did in boot camp. However, I was not getting the results I desired. I was not getting to go home. I then began to lose faith in God. Then, things just kept getting worse. So, I figured God did not care and praying was just a waste of time. I just quit praying.

I felt like I had lost all control of my life. It was like I was at the whim of the universe. I was not getting the sense of peace and relief from prayer like I did in boot camp. Was God testing my faith? Was this any way for me to pass a test? Is this why my prayers were not being answered?

8

WAR PIGS

"Generals gathered in their masses, just like witches at black masses. Evil minds that plot destruction, sorcerers of death's construction. In the fields bodies burning as the war machine keeps turning. Death and hatred to mankind, poisoning their brain washed minds. Oh lord yeah! Politicians hide their tales away. They only started the war. Why don't they go out to fight wars? They leave that all to the poor.

Black Sabbath

The next weeks and days pretty much followed a routine. We built bunkers during the day. At night we sat in our fighting holes watching the horizon for enemy patrols. And in the middle of all of that we trained endlessly for war.

We would wake up in the morning and have three or four neon green scorpions sleeping underneath us. We would catch them in a can or something and make arenas out of the cardboard sleeves that went over the MRE box to keep it closed. Then we would put the scorpions in the ring and stir them up so they would fight. Everyone had their own scorpions. We all bet on them. It was better than Monday night football. The tails on those scorpions would go faster than sewing needles. They would sting each other with out stopping until one of them died. One time we even put in a couple of lizards to see what would happen and the scorpions killed them quickly and then turned on each other. It was like a miniature version of what hell would be like. I remember thinking to myself, "Is this a reminder from God? Is he trying to remind me of what will happen if I completely lose faith in him? Is he trying to give me another chance?" While I was out in the desert, I was becoming so in tune with nature and the things that were going on around me. At times it was as if I had found a way to tap into a new sense that we as humans had lost back in the world.

One time the Lieutenant wanted to get involved in our scorpion betting. So, we let him play with us. He, however, had found the biggest, blackest, scorpion I had ever seen. These scorpions (the black ones) are supposed to be the deadliest scorpions in the world.

"Hey, you can't use that Lieutenant."

"Why not it's a scorpion."

"Yeah but look at the size of that thing. It's not even the same species."

All of ours were the small neon green kind and his was about six inches long and looked like it could stop bullets. So we let him get in on the action and his scorpion killed all ten of ours. We were irritated.

"Damn it Lieutenant, that's not fair."

"I won fair and square now pay up boys."

All ten of us gave him his money. We went to chow. That night a truck came in and brought us lukewarm chow. Finally, we received a meal that did not come out of a bag. I do not know what is worse though, a meal out of a plastic bag or one out of big metal containers made by Marine Corps cooks. We came back after chow and found the Lieutenant's scorpion dead in the ring we built. We all ran over to him.

"Hey Lieutenant, give us our money back".

"What for?"

"Your scorpion is dead in the arena!"

"So what, I still won."

"No way it's a draw sir."

But, to no avail, the Lieutenant would not give us our money back. The next day a water truck with six nozzles on it was sent out to us so that we could take a shower out in the middle of the desert. We had told Staff Sergeant what the Lieutenant did to us the night before. We all lined up in formation and stripped off all of our clothes. We then waited in line to take a shower. Soon we were all done and the Lieutenant was the last to take his shower. While we were all getting dressed Staff Sergeant buried the Lieutenant's clothes in the sand. When he was done showering he went looking for his clothes and we all busted up laughing. Staff Sergeant was rolling with laughter so the Lieutenant went after him. The Staff Sergeant took off running and it was the funniest damn thing I ever saw; the Lieutenant's naked ass chasing Staff Sergeant through the desert. We all said, "That will teach you to fuck with us sir!" Needless to say, the Lieutenant never played with our scorpions and us again.

About once every few weeks we went back to the rear, which were barracks for the oil field workers. It was in

Dhahran. At first it was just the barracks, hot chow, and showers. Then as time went on, they added a PX, fast food restaurants, and a place to watch movies.

One time I was in line for chow and I got up to the food and saw what looked like chili and rice. I said, " What is that, chili?" The cook retorted, "No, it is camel meat with chili sauce over white rice." I started laughing. I thought that was a good joke for over here. I sat down and began to eat. As soon as that first spoon full hit my mouth (I was expecting bland Marine Corps chili) I about barfed and spit my food back onto my tray. "That fucker wasn't joking, that is camel meat. This is the most disgusting shit I ever ate in my life." My buddies all agreed and we went to the PX and got some canned food and Gatorade.

When we stayed overnight in these barracks, it was almost like a vacation for us. One time the whole platoon had a shaving cream fight in the barracks. We were in shower shoes and our shorts and we covered the place with shaving cream. We were sliding and falling all over the place on the floors because they were slick with shaving cream.

While we stayed in the barracks we did our laundry. There were no washing machines so we used to wash our clothes in these big basin sinks they had. We would use shampoo to clean them. The water would be black when we were done. When we took showers we really had to scrub to get all the sand and dried up salt off of us. There would literally be piles of sand on the bottom of the shower when we were done. You would have pounds of sand under your fingernails when you scratched your head.

When we first got out into the desert we were unaware of its inhabitants. We were briefed before hand, but the way things looked we thought we would never see anything. It was so barren; no signs of life anywhere accept ours. The only other signs of life we saw were signs of lives that had expired, such as dead animals. The Saudi people would build these pedestals out of rock. They would then sacrifice an animal, such as a goat or a sheep. They would place the dead animal on top of the rock pedestal. The stench was horrid. The flesh and guts of the animals were rotting in the hot afternoon sun. The flies would feed off of the rotting carcasses. The flies were sick bastards. The landscape looked like a picture of a tropical island with sand and palm trees. The only difference was that the palm trees were rock pedestals with dead, rotting, bloated animals on top of them. Everything here either was dead, dying or living off of the rotting dead flesh of some other pour soul.

One day Laom, a six-foot tall Korean with a stocky build, needed to relieve himself. "Hey, where's the toilet paper at?" Someone tossed him a roll and he disappeared behind a sand knoll. As time went by we noticed Laom had not returned from his nature call. Well, we found out that Laom, while squatting with his pants around his ankles, reached behind himself to get the roll of toilet paper and he got bit by a rattlesnake on top of his hand. Talk about getting caught with your pants down. However, the next day he became famous, for he was on the front page of the military newspaper we used to get. He was listed as the first casualty of the Gulf War. And to top it off the poor guy never even got a purple heart!

While we were out in the desert we were left to fend for ourselves. We had food and water, but they had to be rationed so we would not use them up before we got re-supplied in six months. A lot of the MRE's we received were off of maritime pre-positioning ships. These ships float around with the Navy so that they can supply troops with the things they need if they have to go into battle. So, most of the meals we had were from right after Vietnam, which was the last war the U.S. had been in.

People had dysentery from the poor living conditions we were faced with. You would see Marines walking through the desert and all of a sudden drop their pants and expel a stream of brown water right where they were standing. It was disgusting. Your stomach felt like it was doing back flips constantly and tied in a knot. It felt like you were always extremely nervous. Then, as soon as you would stand up you had to defecate. You had no control over it. It just came out. You had to go right where you were standing. I had it for three months. Some people also got food poisoning and to top it off it was one hundred and thirty degrees during the day.

Once, while I had dysentery, I also came down with food poisoning. I had an MRE in which the cheese that came in it in little packages looked bad. It was all clumpy and separated, but I was so damn hungry that I ate it anyways. That night it was my turn to pull guard duty. It was very late and I was woken up for my shift. I was sweating profusely and had a severe case of the chills. I got up, but I became very light headed so I went to Corporal Zakis, a short Greek fellow with a nose like the little Caesars pizza guy, and told him the situation. He covered my shift for me and I went back to my plot of sand and awaited morning.

When morning broke I went to see the corpsman and he had me lay in the back of the HMMV and stuck an IV into my arm. At that time, because of my dysentery, I had liquid coming out of my hind end, because of the food poisoning I was throwing up and to top it off, because of the intense heat, I was sweating like crazy. I literally had fluid coming out of every orifice of my body. After I received my IV's I had to go back to work.

Every one else was tearing down all of our nets because we were going back to the rear for showers after a long two weeks. I went and sat in the front seat of one of the HMMV's. I then saw Sergeant Martin talk to Corporal Hart who then told me to come over there and get back to work. I was so sick I could not even stand up. I got so angry I said, "Fuck you, I am sick damn it!" And I stayed right where I was. Then, I thought I was going to be in deep trouble for saying that, even if I was half delirious. So I got up and staggered over to join the working party and apologized to Corporal Hart. I told him I was willing to take any punishment he was ready to give me.

By this time our bodies were starting to deteriorate from the horrible living conditions and inadequate nutrition. While this was all occurring, I was fighting another battle in my mind. I had lost all hope, all faith, and I had lost my will to continue. At this point I did not really care if I died. I figured that at least this would be over if I was dead. I felt like I was just alive. I was numb. All I knew was suffering. I had felt like I was completely disarticulated from the real world. It seemed as though we were like misfit toys at Christmas that no one wanted and we were left in some dismal space to eek out our miserable existence. Only, in our world there would be no last minute rescue by Santa Claus.

I often wrote my family about how I was feeling. My letters were brutally honest. To this day I contemplate how my mother must have felt while reading my letters. For one, I am sure she was terrified that I was in a war and then on top of that she had to watch, through my words, my physical and mental decay. She must have felt helpless. I still feel bad about the fact that I had put her through all of that.

Friday September 14, 1990

Dear Mom,

Well, I didn't get your package yet but I got that card with the booger jokes and your letter. I laughed from them jokes. I think that's the first time I've smiled in a month. I'm sure it'll get through I've been getting everyone else's packages and mail. I've been receiving your mail also. I've written you about 4 or 5 times, tell me if your getting my mail. Send me cigarettes please!!!! Don't worry about me smoking that's the least of my worries. Try dodging bullets and shrapnel. Cigarettes aren't shit compared to that. I worry a lot too. I wish I could cry sometimes but I can't it's hard to explain why. I'm through with being strong. I'm sick and tired of my government, my superiors and my own platoon screwing me. I don't give a shit about any damn thing I just don't care no more. I'm so bitter I want to kill the whole world. I don't know how I'll act when I get home but I know you won't like what I am now or who I am. I just role with the punches every day. But I don't think I can take anymore punches mom. If I live through this war my head will be all screwed up. My girl friend will probably dump me, my head will be messed up . I'll basically be screwed what kind of life is that to look forward to when I get out of here? I have nothing to look forward to. All I can see is all my hopes and dreams being shattered as the days go by. Even though I may come home some day, I will never be able to leave this place. That's what sucks. If I'm here to long I just know It'll be my luck she'll dump me mom. It always happens. If I had to face that upon coming from this hole on top of everything else that would be the thing to push me over the edge. Sometimes I think I should just write her a letter and get it over with now so I don't have to face it later but I don't want to lose her, I don't know what to do mom. The good old Marine Corps sure f'd up my life this time. God this place sucks! Yesterday I got put on shit detail. We've got these wooden boxes we shit in and in the bottom is a 55 gallon oil drum that's cut in half that everything goes into. You have to pull the drum out from a little door in the back and poor diesel fuel in it. Then you light the shit on fire. And you've got to stir it until It burns away. Then you take the sediment that's left and dump it out and bury it. That's just an idea of some of the things they do to us here. They treat us like we're two-year-old nobodys that don't know how to do a damn thing. They told us that on October 15 we are supposed to go into offensive combat and attack the Iraqis. I say they just should nuke the assholes and send us home. None of us get hardly no sleep at all either. I could fall asleep jogging right now I'm so tired the thing about the flag stamp is bullshit I get all your letters so far. I don't know what the paper said about our daily routine but I'm sure they lied and the only troops they talk to are troops that are in the rear. I'm in the desert not in no air conditioned building. Plus they can't tell you how bad it really is because the government won't let them. Besides there ain't no reporter crazy enough to come out in 130 degree desert by the border and interview us. So don't believe everything the paper say's about what we do. I've read a few of those articles and they lie a lot. They make it sound like we don't have it too bad out here. Well how does one shower every two weeks sound to you! They wont tell you stuff like that and it pisses me off! Just send magazines or articles pertaining to my situation here we don't get any news. I don't know what the hell is going on in the real world. And send lots of Marlboro red cigarettes please! It's the only thing I've got out here. Send me a walkman with AA batteries that has a tape player and a radio. Because my walkman broke and I need to listen to some damn thing. Don't worry they don't search through the mail. You can send what ever you want don't make the packages to big that's all. I got a letter from Jerry today also. He's such a good friend! He feels bad that I'm over here and he's sitting at college. He said if war breaks out he's gonna join. I don't want to see him throw away his life over here. He's got too much going for him. There's too much pain and suffering here. He wouldn't be able to finish college when he got back he'd be to mentally messed up. That's what I'm here fighting for. So he can have a trouble free future and make the best of his life. So please don't let him make a stupid mistake like that!! Please!! Don't believe the rumors mom. It's to late I've lost all faith. It does no good to have any anyway's. It just lets you down all the time! Well I've got to go now. I love you all very much, tell tom and Amanda I said hi and I love them too.

Love you all a lot,
Robert

Friday, September 21, 1990

Dear Mom, Tom and Amanda,
I am getting your mail and everyone's package

except my girlfriend's package she sent it about 3 or 4 weeks ago and I still haven't got it. I wonder why? She signed her letter I got from her yesterday like this: Love Hopefully soon Mrs Jade Serocki. I thought that was kind of cute. I feel bad that I had to leave her and put her through this but I guess I'll be home with her soon, I hope! Well what are you guys up to? Same old shit here, there's nothing really to say except I want to come home now with out having to go to war. I love you guys and I miss ya and I can't wait to see ya!

Love,
Robert

Monday, September 24, 1990

Dear Mom, Tom and Amanda,
Hi, how you all doing? Me, well I'm pretty shitty, I suppose you could guess why! I got your package and your bitch joke card yesterday. Thank you! It was great! Everyone laughed at the jokes! I know your going through hell there too but at least you don't have to dodge bullets! And you also have your husband and people you love with you, I have nothing! They are getting us ready to attack Kuwait in October some time. I think war is inevitable. Besides I'm so pissed off I'm personally going to get a piece of Saddam's ass! You'll see, because I'm gonna cut his balls off and feed them to him and then I'm gonna take that rag off of his head and bring it home and hang it above my T.V. and throw darts at it!!!! Besides that there's nothing else really to say except that I hope I come home soon too, unharmed of course! Tom tell all the guys at work I said thanks and not to change

there minds once we roll into Kuwait and they start sending American soldiers home in body bags! There has been 26 deaths over here so far. All of them Army. The French Foreign Legion and the British Royal Marines want to fight by our side because of our ass kicking reputation. I'll write again soon.

Love you all lots,
Robert

While we were in a defensive status, the first six months we were in country, we used to move around a lot. Usually, we moved to a new location every ten days to two weeks. When we did move to a new location we would set up camie nets to camouflage our vehicles, like the HMMV's and Amtracks (amphibious tracked vehicles that carry about thirty to forty troops and are made completely out of metal). Then we would dig our individual fighting holes. This is where we would sleep.

These fighting holes were also placed under the cami-netting. The holes had to be armpit deep and about long enough to lie down in. It was like getting a preview of what death was like and what it was going to feel like being put six foot under when we were buried after we died. It really put things into perspective. I remember lying there at night thinking, "Is this what death will be like? No sole, no breath, alone in the ground staring up at the sky for eternity."

Every time we dug those holes I would remember what my dad always used to tell me, "If you don't get an education son, you'll be digging ditches for the rest of your life!" I used to get perturbed every time that little voice in my head repeated it while I was digging ditches to live in.

Sometimes, I thought down in a hole in the ground, several thousands of miles from home I figured out what life was about. To do whatever you want with it. After all, it is yours. Do what ever makes you happy, because you are the one who has to live with it, not anybody else. Right then and there I promised myself that if I made it home I was going to do what ever I wanted with my life and I was going to enjoy it, especially if God gave me a second chance and let me live through this.

I had to get my faith back. I had to believe God would help me. I started thinking this would be the only way to make it out of here. I had to have faith. Things were bad and kept getting worse as if something was forcing me to believe or totally give up. I was actually scared that if I gave up I would die. I thought that God continued giving me chances to regain my faith in him and one day he would quit. I did not want to end up there.

One day we stopped in a location that actually contained very few, but some, live bushes. They were the size of basketballs. I thought, "Great, a sign of life!" After disembarking the Amtracks and stepping into the beach like sand, I noticed the area was covered with sheep excrement. It was everywhere. It looked like someone went to the beach and dumped cocoa puffs all over the sand. It was disgusting.

"Are we really gonna stay here Staff Sergeant?"

"Yes, we are."

"Can't we just move over a few meters or something to get out of all of this sheep shit?" "No, this is our position we will just have to live with it. Besides, once you dig your hole you will be below the sheep shit and you wont have to worry about it."

I went about my business digging my hole and cursing this God-forsaken country. I thought that God must have really hated this place. It was eerie here. It was like I had stepped back in time. This place was like the spawning ground of the Devil himself.

Every scoop of sand I dug contained sheep feces. "This place is like the world's biggest fucking kitty litter box. There's nothing here but sand, shit and bugs that eat shit!" I finally got armpit deep, which is about five feet for me, and much to my amazement, the bottom of my hole still had sheep dung in it. "Son of a bitch! I dug five fucking feet under the ground and there still is sheep shit here. The sheep must have been shitting here since the biblical times!" Everyone laughed at what I had said. Needless to say I did not enjoy sleeping here.

That night when I went to bed, I placed my sleeping mat in the bottom of the hole and I wrapped myself up tight with my poncho liner like a burrito so no dung would get in while I was sleeping. My gear was all piled on top of my pack so It would not be in the sand and touching the sheep dung. I had my poncho tied up to the cami-netting on the side of my hole to block the wind from blowing sand and sheep dung on me.

I woke up in the morning and I was covered with little balls of sheep dung. It was everywhere. I felt so dirty. It was disgusting. I wanted to burn every thing I owned and scrub myself with bleach, scouring powder and a wire brush. However, I could not. I had to suck it up and deal with it. I did not complain about it because it did not matter. We were not leaving this spot for a few days.

I never worried too much about washing my hands and stuff like that back at the base in the U.S. You could get clean anytime, but out here I felt like a little kid again. I felt helpless. I could not clean myself or take care of myself the way I was taught. That little voice in my head kept tormenting me again, repeating the words of my mother. "Don't touch that you don't know where its been. Wash your hands before you eat. Get in the bath right now mister!"

My brain was telling me to clean myself and take care of myself like my mother had taught me, but I could not do anything about it. My brain kept repeating these things over and over again. Not only was it a battle to survive over here, but there was a battle raging inside my mind between trying to get me to do what I was taught since childhood, acting like a wild animal to survive, and the testing of my faith!

One day, about mid-afternoon, we saw a group of camels, a mother and several young ones, meandering through the desert. So me and some other guys went over to the camels with some crackers from the MRE's. We began feeding them to the camels. They really seemed to enjoy them. They were slobbering all over our hands. They reminded me of one of those dogs with the big jowls that ooze with slime and when they shake their heads slop flies everywhere. We were having a bit of fun feeding the camels as well.

Then, as soon as we ran out of crackers the mother camel became violent. She started snorting at us, then spitting at us. "What the fuck", I shouted. "We give you disgusting fucking animals some of our food and this is the thanks we get for helping you out!" At that moment I began to wonder if this was foreshadowing how the Arabic people were going to treat us. "I sure hope not!" After this incident, we finally went back to the rear again for showers.

Once we got back and settled in, we decided to get some chow. "Hey Serocki, lets go to the PX and get some real food and cigarettes." "Ok." So Sven and I were off to

A Line In the Sand

the PX. We were not allowed to carry our weapons with us. This was probably so they would not have any pre-mature Arab deaths. However, I carried my knife with me. The blade itself was about six inches long. It put Rambo's knife to shame. By this time we had been here for a little over two months and most of us were angry about being here and we wanted to get home. Our motto was, "If you want to fight a damn war then lets fight the son of a bitch, otherwise let us go back home damn it!"

On the way through the oil field barracks we always passed a mosque, where the Arabs worshipped Allah. So, this time while walking by I became overcome with anger and shouted "Fuck you cock sucking Arabs!" and I hocked the biggest loogie I ever hocked onto the front steps of the so-called place of worship. I then said, "Worship that Mother-Fuckers!"

We finally made it to the PX. It was like a shopping mall now. They had a little grocery section with canned foods and the like, reminiscent of a drug store. They also had an area where they sold tapes and radios. They even had a barbershop set up! "How ironic was this? The Saudi's were making money off of us while we protected them. If that don't take the cake", I thought.

So we went over to the food section and bought some Gatoraide, cigarettes, and some Spreadables. The Spreadables were cans of tuna or chicken with mayo and relish. We thought they were the best things since sliced bread. We would eat the stuff right out of the can! Then, Sven wanted to buy a radio. So we went over to the so-called electronics isle and he looked at little transistor radios and I looked at tapes. All they had were oldies, but that was what we all listened to anyways, along with heavy metal music.

Sven bought a tiny little transistor radio for us to listen to in the desert in hopes that we could stay in touch with the world while everything passed us by, unbeknownst to us. It was like we were stuck in a time warp at a certain period in time and everything else was moving along and progressing without us and we did not know it even happened. It seemed like we would be here for the rest of our lives.

Just then, this Saudi gentleman walked up to me and introduced himself and grabbed my hand and got two inches from my face. He started talking to me and professed his appreciation for us defending his country and its people. It was scary at first. I am not used to people being that close to my face while they are talking to me, except for boot camp, but they were not really talking to us then.

He also held on to my hand the whole time he talked to me. I also noticed that he shook my right hand with his right hand and he did not touch me with the left one. I noticed a lot of Saudi's not doing things with their left hands. We were told this is because a person's left hand is considered the dirty hand and is used only for wiping your derrière and other things of that nature. I thought that having to worry about what hand I use for a specific task was a little vacuous. However, it also reminded me of how impetuous Americans can be at times. I figured he was probably thinking the same way about me. "Man, this place is fucking weird", I thought. We then left and headed back to our humble abode, the oil field barracks, where we would pig out on what we called real food, compared to the post Vietnam era MRE's we had grown so accustomed to.

During this time, my mental and physical state deteriorated further. I really began to develop a very deep resentment and hatred toward the Middle East and its people. My girlfriend had quit writing me. My parents were upset about who was receiving more letters than the other. They knew I was not doing well and they were riding their own emotional roller coaster. I actually contemplated to quit writing letters to them. My uncle would fill his letters with words of wisdom and positive reinforcement. Sometimes the words he wrote would help and other times they would not. I exemplified these things when I wrote to them. In the beginning of our tour over here I loved to write and receive letters. At this junction of my duty assignment in the desert, I felt like writing letters was just something I had to do. I really did not want to write, nor did I care.

October 2, 1990

Dear Uncle Dennis,
Thanks for the magazine! It helped take my mind off things for a while. Tell Dana and Mary I said hi! I've received a letter from Dana already. Ya I suppose I'll have to clean up Detroit too! If I see any damn Arabs when I get home they'll definitely be hamburger. I'm doing ok I guess I'm just sick and tired of living like a damn cannibal, spoiled food, no showers, the shits, crotch rot, always too damn hot and humid, there's no relief. I can't wait to come home eat a decent meal, take a shower, and have an ice cold beer! That's all for now. Later,
Love,
Robert

October 2, 1990

Dear Mom,
It was good to hear your voice and Tom's. I got

a letter from you yesterday thanks. There's not much to say mom. I'm doing alright I guess. I'm sick and tired living like an animal. Damn these flies are really starting to piss me the hell off. There's hundreds of them landing on my face my lips every damn where. And they wont go away. There's dead animals and trash every where out here and we live right in the middle of it. God it sucks here damn it I want to come home. They told us that we cant think about home no more basically we can't love nobody. We're here now and we don't need any moral problems. The colonel said that once we even start thinking about our families and friends we'll be the one's who die first! Well I've got to try and find some shade now. I'll write again soon!
    Love,
    Robert

October 6, 1990, 11:20AM

Dear Mom, Tom and Amanda,
I received all three of your packages, food, cigarettes, and the walkman. Thanks a lot, I was like a kid at X-mas. Those tapes were awesome you sent. Tom bought those huh? Send a couple more not too many though, I won't be able to carry all those tapes. Well my girlfriend hasn't written me in 18 days now. I wonder what the hell her deal is, maybe she's got a good excuse, who knows with my luck she probably met someone else and forgot about me. I hope not. God is it humid here. At night when the winds stop water drips down on me from our cammi net like rain because it gets so humid. My cammies have mold on them because I never dry off between the sweat and humidity. God

those damn fly's really piss me off, they never leave you alone. I can't understand why they want to land on me when they got plenty of decent camel shit to play with. God this country is messed up. This is not a place for a honey moon that's for sure. I didn't think there was such a place as BFE (Bum Fuck Egypt) well, I've found it, literally. Tell Tom and Mandy May I said hello and I love them. I love you too mom. Take care!

Love ya,
Robert

October 16, 1990

Dear Aunt Sandy,
Maybe I'll get lucky and be there when Mary and Ron get there in February because I'm sure gramps will be good for a few laughs. Tell Uncle Dennis I said happy birthday. Tell him to look on the bright side, he didn't have to spend his birthday in Saudi Arabia especially his 21st birthday like I will probably have to. Well I just wanted to say thanks for the package and the words of wisdom I could use them I explained to Uncle Dennis in his letter about what happened with me so just have him fill ya in. Don't worry about me I'm to hard for these assholes! I just got over the flu today. I was sicker than hell for two days in the sweltering heat no less. God did that suck but I'm better now. Well I've got to go now so take care.

Love,
Robert

October 16, 1990

Dear Uncle Dennis,
I got your letter and Aunt Sandy's letter and

package. Thanks, but don't send stamps anymore because I can mail things for free now ok. I was upset but I didn't say for you guys to not write me. What I told my mom was I wasn't gonna write her because she was complaining to my dad because he gets more letters than she does, well he's gonna because he writes me more often than she does. And I said until she matures some and stops playing these stupid little games with me then I'll write to her. But I have been writing her. I had a bad day that day and my girlfriend hasn't written in 28 days now. As far as what you said thanks. I could really use the advice in the shitty situation I'm in but don't get the wrong Idea I'm ok. I just have my shitty day's out here which is to be expected. Well I've got to go now. Hey Uncle Dennis, you're the greatest too!!!!

Love,
Robert

October 16, 1990

Dear Mom,

Well, today I just got over food poisoning for the second time, god was I sick and the heat made it twice as bad. Other than that I'm ok. You shouldn't let your nerves get to you like that mom. You know what I mean? No they are not rotating us in 3 months and they are not giving us leave in Germany. Hell I'm not in the Army or the Air Force! When we do leave we'll be the last to leave. We're the front line troops. Like the saying goes "First to go last to leave." They're saying we'll be here until February and since we'll be the last to rotate we'll probably leave in March or April, what

a bunch of bullshit! Well not much else to say except take care and I'm hot as hell! Tell Tom to send another of his tapes (Super Tramp) send me some Raman noodles and some Sternos to cook them with ok. Love you guys.
Love ya,
Robert

October 18, 1990

Dear Mom,
I haven't got much time so a quick note: Nice to hear yours and Toms voice again! Don't use the new address I gave you they weren't supposed to tell to use it yet so use the one you've been using from San Francisco. And send that tape recorder so I can make a tape and not have to use the Lieutenants tape recorder.
Bye!
Love,
Robert
P.S. Got a letter from you and grandma today. You said Carl Parker shot himself. Didn't anybody hear it? I'm sure that's not a regular occurrence over there.

October 22, 1990

Dear Mom,
I got your card the other day, thanks. Ya, when I come home we'll all have to watch those movies together, I'd like to see them! Today it was 100 degrees and 100% humidity and we had to wear our gas masks and suits for an hour. God did I sweat my ass off! I'm still sweating and it's 5:11PM at night, god

this place sucks! I can't wait to come home! I'm basically ok. I'm just sick and tired of livin like an animal. Well time to go love you all!

Love Robert

October 27, 1990

Dear Mom,

Just a quick note, not much time. I got a letter from you a couple of days ago. We all wish that they would shit or get off the pot also! So her teacher cried huh? Ask her if it's ok when I get back I'd like to spend a half a day or something with the kids in Amanda's class to show them that I care about them also! I would sure like to see there smiling faces and hear their laughter and watch them as they play without a worry in the world and think to myself I made it possible for them to be so carefree and happy because of the things that I sacrificed for them. I tell ya mom there's nothing in this world that beats that feeling of knowing that I may have to sacrifice my life for hundreds of people and kids so they can live their life carefree and the way they want too! Mom, that's a true American, I feel so good about what I am doing I get goose bumps and my eyes water. Mom, why do I care so much about people and things I don't know and who would rather shit on me than help me? I guess I've got your caring heart mom. I may have been selfish about other things but I am making the biggest most unselfish sacrifice of all! And I know you'd be proud of me. It's just to bad not too many people appreciate what I am doing for them. But I am not doing this to get any thing in return. All I want is to be able

to see there happy faces when this is all over and know that I made those smiles possible! Thank you mom for all that you tried to teach me when I was growing up. I know now and believe that no matter who teaches you or what they teach you it isn't as important as what your mother teaches you because no one cares or worry's about you as much as your mother does. I'm sorry I am putting you through this mom but it's something I have to do. I'm sure you understand. Well, I've got to go now.
    Love ya Lots,
    Robert

During this time, I was making tapes for my parents with my Lieutenant's tape recorder. They would do the same and send them back to me so I could hear their voices. It was nice because it helped me to feel like I was not missing too much while I was in the desert. My girlfriend had quit writing me and I was hurt. I ran into Klark again. I asked him if he still had his Tarot cards and he did. So I had asked him to perform another reading for me. He agreed. I asked about my girlfriend. Klark looked at his cards and told me that I would be getting a letter from her in about two weeks. Then he said it would probably be more like ten days. He also told me that I would meet someone else when I got back from the war and that I would end up marrying her. However, he said that my parents would not approve and we would end up breaking up. He said we could try to make it work, but chances are that it would not work out. I became elated that I was finally going to hear from my girlfriend again. The ten days had finally passed and I had forgotten what Klark and his Tarot cards had told me. Sure enough, just like Klark had said, I received a letter from her. However, it was the last letter I wrote to her. It was returned to me with a label on it. The label said, "Return to sender, not at this address." She had moved or something and did not even bother to tell me.

9

WHICH WAY ARE YOU GOING?

"Which way are you going? Which side will you be on? Will you stand and watch while the seeds of hate are sewn? Will you stand with those who say, there's will be done? One hand on the bible, one hand on the gun.

by Jim Croce

In November I had been transferred to Headquarters Platoon. I was assigned to my Captain. My new job required another Marine from the heavy equipment platoon and myself to drive a C-tractor. This tractor had a big scoop on the front of it and a backhoe bucket on the back. We drove this machine around and dug fighting holes and trenches for everyone in the platoon and when we moved, which was every three days, we filled them in. We did this by day and stood our share of guard duty at night. When I first got assigned to the C-tractor I stayed in the same area with the First Sergeant and his driver Lance Corporal Hahn. The First Sergeant was in Vietnam so we felt comfortable with him.

One day, Hahn was driving the First Sergeant around in the HMMV and I was with them. I was sitting in the back seat. It was about one o'clock in the afternoon and this family of Arabs had pulled off the side of the highway, which was to our left. We were driving through the desert. They were praying to Allah. The woman was unveiled. When this happens it is very bad for the women to be seen by anybody else without the veil on. So, as we drove by we honked the horn and waived and she looked up at us and we saw her without the veil. Her husband became very upset and starting yelling in Arabic and grabbed her by the scruff of the neck and drug her over to the Chevrolet Suburban they had and threw her in. We all had a good laugh about that one. We did not care. This place sucked and we had to be here so our motto was "fuck 'em." Shortly after that I was assigned to stay with the Captain.

The Captain also had a driver, who was Bails. I knew him well. We were good friends. He was in my company. When we were not operating the C-tractor, I started to exercise. I took a camie-net pole and filled two coffee cans with sand. I ran rope through the tops of them and hung them on each end of the pole so it was like a barbell. I lifted weights like I used to do back in the real world. I tried to make this place as much like home as I could. I even got Bails to start working out.

One day the Captain came up to me and said, "You're a good Marine Serocki. You came over here with me and you've been doing a great job and even got Bails to start working out." I felt good and it helped me to stay positive. I felt like it was up to me to keep those around me motivated and it was at that point that I decided that I would have to just accept death. I was tired of being afraid of death. I figured if it was my destiny to die here then so be it. I was not going to worry about it any more.

It was at this time that my faith in God really became strong. I said my prayers every night and talked to God constantly throughout the day. It was a release for me of my worries and helped me to somehow feel like I had some sort of control over my destiny. I became so faithful that I started to think that maybe I had gone crazy, maybe I cracked up and had lost control. I was so worried about it, that on a tape I made for my dad, I told him of my new found faith and I told him that I hoped that I had not gone crazy. But, I had to have some kind of hope. Hope was the only thing that kept me going, the only thing that made me want to get out of this place and live. I finally just decided that whatever had happened to me, whether I was crazy or not, that I would continue with it because it was working for me. It helped me to get through each day and keep a positive attitude. In a way it was like I had turned the corner on this whole war thing and I was now starting my journey home, whether it was in a jet plane or in a body bag. I had made my peace with God and I felt I could get on with my duties without having to worry. It was as if I had passed his test of my faith and he was rewarding me again.

As I mentioned earlier, I made a tape for my dad. We still wrote each other, but now we also had tapes of each other to listen to. It helped a lot to have those. I could not wait to receive them in the mail. All of my friends listened to them with me. It was a piece of home for us all. They even talked on my tapes back to my parents. So we had a little bit of technology with us. We even had a video camera in the company.

One day the Captain borrowed the video camera and he pulled me aside. He asked me if I would videotape him so he could send a message to his wife and I agreed. He sat down on a gas can or something and I turned the camera on. I will never, for as long as I live, forget what happened next. He pulled out a birth certificate with his newborn son's footprints on it. His wife had a child while he was over here in hell. My heart sunk into my stomach. I kept filming. He made a message for his wife and at the end he said, holding up his son's birth certificate, "This is why I am doing this honey, for this little guy." He then started crying and said he was done. This was unheard of. A Marine Corps Captain crying in front of one of his Lance Corporals. At that moment, I knew that he had a lot of trust in me, and thought that I was a good enough Marine to do what I did for him and it was ok for him to cry in front of me. From that moment on, I had the deepest respect for that man, deeper than I ever had for anyone in my life. He was a human being just like me and at that moment we were equals. I felt like we really bonded that day. I turned off the camera and walked up to him. He said,

"Sorry, Serocki."

"Don't worry about sir, you're only human. I have more respect for you now than I ever did and I would follow you straight through the gates of hell....sir!"

I then shook his hand. He said,

"Thank you, Serocki."

"Your welcome, sir."

All of us, no matter what rank you were, really began to bond. We all had our reasons to fight and live. We shared those with each other. I never have felt such a strong bond with human beings in my life. We were all hurting inside. I finally realized that I was not alone in my feelings of despair. I was ok.

One morning, upon waking up we were given the order to tear down the nets and fill in the trenches and holes. We were moving. So, while everyone was taking things down, me and the guy from heavy equipment, filled in holes with the C-tractor. My partner was from Texas, he was new to the Corps. Although I never asked, he did not look a day over eighteen. He was a Private First Class. I just called him Texas.

We finally got everything filled in and we were all lining our vehicles up in a single file row in order to move to the new location. We were located at the very end. We kept a good deal of distance between each of us in case of attack from the air or where ever. Shortly after starting out, Texas and I heard a loud bang and all of a sudden the C-tractor just quit moving. "What the fuck was that?", Texas shouted. At first we thought we hit a land mine or something. We piled out of the truck and tried to asses the damage. We figured we were not in a minefield or we would have blown up. There was no smoke or anything like that.

We looked up in front of the tractor, which is where the noise came from. We discovered that we blew a U-joint. We could not drive anymore. By this time, the rest of the convoy had moved on and we had no radio. We could not contact anyone. We were out in the middle of the desert. We had no food. All we had was our rifles, ammo and two canteens of water.

"What the fuck do we do now Serocki?"

"We just sit tight and wait. I am sure once they get where

they are going they will realize we are missing and they will come back for us."

"How long do you think that will be?"

"Well, probably not until morning."

"Holy shit! What about food?"

"We will be fine just relax. I think I may have some crackers or something so don't worry."

Nighttime soon approached and no one had come back for us yet. I told Texas that we would have to stand guard duty through the night. I told him I would take the first four-hour watch and he could take the second. It soon became dark and we saw a vehicle approaching with running lights on. We could not be sure who it was.

"Texas lock and load your weapon and get behind a tire."

"Holy fuck! Who's coming?"

"I don't know yet so be prepared to fucking rock and roll Marine!"

We waited for a vehicle to approach. The vehicle stopped. My heart was pounding. Sweat started to bead up on forehead and roll down my face. I had to stay calm. I was the senior Marine here and I had to take charge.

I saw some people get out of the vehicle and approach. I still could not tell if it was friend or foe. They could be Marines, so I figured I better not just open up fire. I had to take a chance and halt them. If they were Iraqis, yelling would mark us and we would lose our surprise. However, it had to be done. They could be Marines.

"Halt Mother-Fucker or I'll blow your testicles back to the Stone Age!"

"We are fellow Americans. We came back to find you guys."

I could tell by their English they were Americans. I told Texas to stay put just in case and I got out to greet them and sure enough they were Marines. We loaded into their vehicle and they took us back to camp. We would have to come back out in the morning with the new part and fix the C-tractor then. I wrote home to tell my parents about my new job.

November 3, 1990

Dear Mom,

I got your package yesterday and your card today thanx. Ya it's still a standoff in other words boring as hell! I guess you could say we're all pretty nuts by now. Don't get your hopes up too high about Christmas because I seriously don't think I'll be home before February or March at least, maybe even longer. Just because I was one of the first troops here doesn't mean I'll be the first one to come home. Remember I'm a Marine and Marines are the first to go and last to leave because we are the only ones that can do the job! We don't give up! And this mission has proved that to the president! The tapes were great and I've used the toilet paper quite extensively it's like royalty to have toilet paper. Around here if you've got it your everybody's friend! Ha ha I may not like the way the Marine Corps does things or why they do things or the things they do but I'm so glad that I joined because I have learned so many valuable lessons about life and I've learned so much about myself I wouldn't trade this experience in for anything. I've seen so many other cultures and I've seen how lucky we are to live in the good ol' US of A and how good we have it. I'm even glad I'm going through this experience now. Even though I hate it and I want to come home I've learned a lot about myself here. I learn so much every day here. I now know I am in the worst possible situation in life and I'm making it and I will make it. So no matter what kind of shit life throws my way I know I'll make it through it. Mentally I've become very strong and those lessons are so valuable I would never trade it in for anything. And I don't regret the decision I made back on February 10th when I said "I do, so help me god." One thing about myself you may or may not know. It could be a very good point but it could also be a fault. I don't know where I get it from but I can't stand to lose, I always have to win! I can't stand to have somebody better than me. No matter how much it hurts no matter how much pain and agony I go through I always push myself to the max 150% all the time. Like when we run If I don't come in first I feel like shit and I get pissed off so I go out and practically kill myself training to be number one! Then the next time we run I come in first and I feel awesome, you can't beet that feeling mom. Knowing you are the best and that is one of the reasons I joined the Marine Corps, because they are the best! And everyone around the world knows it! Why do you think Saddam Hussein won't cross the border or why he doesn't want war? Because on the other side of the border there is 30,000 Marines that would love the chance to kick his ass and wouldn't stop short of him getting slaughtered! And he knows it. And the British soldiers know it too! That's why they told the Army to go to hell and they came and joined are forces and now they are under Marine Corps command. Sometimes my hard work pays off. The other day I got a new job for 2 or 3 weeks. The Captain called my staff sergeant and said I want Serocki to come work for me for 2 or 3 weeks and my staff sergeant said, "Why Serocki?" and the captain said, "Just have him here by Saturday." So Saturday I came out here and I operate a C tractor. It has a bucket on the front for digging big holes and it has a scoop on the back for digging trenches. It's made by Mercedes Benz. I drive it around and I operate the bucket and the scoop and get this it's a stick shift ha ha. Its really easy and it gets me away from my staff sergeant for a while thank god. My address is still the same so don't worry. Well I'll close for now. I love you mom and I love Tom and Amanda too!

Take care, Lots of love,
Robert

November 7, 1990

Dear Uncle Dennis,

Not much going on over here. We're just scaring the living shit out of Saddam (sand nigger) Hussein! I always love to get your letters they always put me in tears cause I laugh so damn hard at some of the things you come up with, thanks! They told us in 2 to 3 weeks we'll know what month were getting rotated in. I figure it will be in February or march knowing these fuck sticks we've got for leaders! I hope he does pull out of Kuwait for his sake because if I have to go in there slinging lead I'm gonna personally torture Saddam twice as bad as he is doing to the U.S. hostages and then I'm gonna kick his mother fucking ass until I'm positive he's dead (which may take a lot of convincing!) and then I'm gonna take his shirt off so he's bare chested and I'm gonna take my arab sticker and carve U.S.M.C. in his chest then I'm gonna pour gas in the letters and hang him in the town square and light the gas on fire with my last match and then for kicks I'll light a cigarette from the flames and I'll sit there and laugh and then I'll commend myself on how good of a job I did! After that the whole arab world including Mohammed the holy sandnigger will know who Eddie Sedutski is! Ha ha pretty good huh? Well, take care!

Love,
Robert

November 12, 1990

Dear Mom,

I got your card the other day. So Amanda is starting to ask some pretty good questions huh? The other day I was telling my buddy about that time on Halloween when that guy scared the shit out of me. He laughed. I wish I was there again. I have been here 3 months on November 14th and It may be a lot longer because they are talking about going to war and they are bringing all of the troops over here now. They have to decide on it this month because next month the U.N. jurisdiction goes to a country called Yemin who is Iraq's only friend and they would never allow a war to happen and basically screw everything up we've worked so hard to accomplish. I hope we do go attack cause I'm pissed off especially since he's starving all those hostages that's bullshit. There's a movie called "Born on the 4th of July" It'll remind you of me cause I did the same things and had the same dreams when I was a kid. I was in awe with the Marine Corps and I joined for the same reasons he did. Watch it you can rent it it's on video now. And write me and tell me what you think. Well take care! Love ya!
Robert

P.S. If we do go to war I may not have time to write you so don't get scared if we go in and you don't get a letter from me ok?
Love ya,
Robert

November 13, 1990

Dear Uncle Dennis,
I've gotten all your mail, you know not to use the new address any more right? Well don't ok. My squad leader goofed up when he told us to use it. Today we are having a bitchin sand storm! 50 mile and hour winds with sand flying everywhere what a hell hole this place is! I still write mom, I realized what you said after what I wrote her and the next day I wrote a letter to her and apologized to her. So your thinking of getting a four wheel drive huh? That's cool. I'll have to help you break it in when I come home, whenever the hell that is. I'm doing pretty good today besides the fact I've got a pound of sand in my ass! So how are you doing? Yesterday me and two of my buddies made a barbell out of a pole and two sand bags, pretty neet huh? Hey I've got a pretty good farmers tan going! Well, take care.
I love ya,
Robert

November 21, 1990

Dear Uncle Dennis,
Hey thanks for the cookies, they arrived in excellent shape. I've gotten a couple of letters from you but I've been to busy to write lately. The MRE's suck!

And so does the chow they serve! I've had food poisoning 3 times since I've been here so fuck that dumb old fucken general he don't know what it's like to be a troop anyhow! I started to get down cause of thanksgiving then I said hey wait a minute I do have something to be thankful for........I'm still alive! So I'm ok for now. Have a good holiday! Your more like my best buddy than my uncle. I look forward to spending time with you. I always wanted to call you up and see if I could stay the weekend at your house but I didn't want to impose you know what I mean? Hopefully when I get home we can spend a lot more time together than we used too. Thanks for all the great memories! Take care, I love you guy's a lot!
Love,
Robert

November 22, 1990

Dear Mom, Tom and Amanda,

Happy Thanksgiving! Ya, we've been doing a lot of weird shit out here in the desert. You're right we are a dedicated bunch but we have to be, that's why we are always so successful. About shitting behind furniture I don't remember why I used to do that but I used to pee in my drawers at night because I was so scared of the dark and the hallway was to dark to walk down so I'd pee in my desk drawer. I wish I could come home so bad. Yesterday I just about cut my finger off with my knife! It's almost as big as a sword and sharp as hell. Well I was cutting some card board with it for the captain and I slipped and cut my finger. It bled pretty good but I got the bleeding to stop so now I'm ok. That's about all for now so have a good holiday I wish I was there but I have a job to finish

mom so I'll be home when it's done. I love you guys bunches. Especially you Amanda you're my little buddy!
Take care,
Love ya Lots,
Robert

November 27, 1990

Dear Uncle Dennis,
I got your book on positive thinking yesterday, thanks. I'm doing good. How about yourself? Well another day has passed so now I'm one day closer to home! Son of a bitch it's starting to rain here. What a freak of nature! Well I just wanted to say thanks and let you know I'm doing a ok! So you take care and take it easy.
Love,
Robert

November 29, 1990

Dear Mom,
I got your tree the other day, thanks. I was at the Marine Corps birthday but each batallion had there own. I could have been on the news, but I don't know for sure. I don't pay attention to those assholes anyway's cause all they do is lie, they'll never tell you what it's really like. Our officers won't let us tell them either. We have to act like were fucking happy here! Ya right. They don't explain to you what it's like not being able to sleep at night cause your afraid, you get this feeling it's some kind of feeling as if you were going to the hospital for open heart surgery. There's dead camels and goats all over that are half rotten and

smell like hell! There's hundreds of fly's and shit beetles everywhere, trash the saudi's just dump where ever they please! They don't tell you about the shitty food or about when you scratch your head and get ten pounds of dirt under your fingernails because you haven't showered in days. Today the NBC (nuclear biological chemical) officer was telling us about things we are going to get in case we get gassed with a nerve agent. They have nothing for mustard gas, you just pray you don't turn into one big puss bucket! They are gonna give us these little pills we are supposed to take that increase our chances of not being affected by nerve gas by 14% then after those if we feel the symptoms of a nerve agent then we have these auto injectors (shots) we give ourselves in the thigh with needles so big you can look down through the hole at the end of the needle and see the other side! Then if we start going into convulsions our buddy has to give us a shot of valume to slow down our impulses from our nerves to mellow you out otherwise your brain gets fried, you'll be alive but you'll have no memory but you'll be a vegetable the rest of your life! We don't have that many corpsman here so we all have learned first aid and if your buddy gets shot or blown to shit you have to patch him up and then leave him there and go on in hopes that a medivac will pick him up later. God all that blood, I cant take this shit! They said you may have 4 or 5 guys wounded and you come up to your buddy who is unconscious and is not breathing, you have no time to do CPR and try to save him or if he's wounded very badly you have no time to save him you have to leave him and try to save the guys who have a fighting chance! I could never leave a bleeding friend to die like that, god sometimes I don't know what the hell I'm gonna do. I can see it now , running up on one of my buddys who just had both of his legs blown off and he's screaming help me, help please and according to these assholes I have to turn my head and walk the other way. God I pray so hard that we don't go to war, I just want to come home and make this all a bad dream! Gosh, I love you guys so much I hope everybody is grateful for what I'm doing or may have to do here, even when body bags start coming home full. They've got them here I've already seen them. God mom I hate to admit it but I'm scared.

Love ya lots,
Robert

At this point, I started receiving letters from a girl in Arizona. She had obtained my name and address off of a list that was compiled by the Red Cross and sent out to various businesses. We wrote over the course of my tour of duty in the Gulf. We fell in love with each other through the mail without ever having actually met. I had a picture of her. She was tiny, about five-foot six inches tall. She had long blond hair and her name was Meggan. We planned on getting together when I returned home from the war. Her letters gave me a new hope and a new sense of purpose.

It was also during this time that our government, in their infinite wisdom, started testing out various pills and vaccinations on us. They had nerve agent pills, anthrax pills, and botchelism shots. We had a cocktail of untested drugs to eat everyday. They even told us that these pills and vaccinations were untested and the FDA had not even seen them yet. They would put us into formation and make us take the pills. They would tell us that it was up to us if we wanted to take the pills, but that we would want to take them. I used to throw them over my shoulder. The only pills I took were the little green nerve agent pills. They were supposed to increase our chances of survival from a nerve agent attack by fourteen percent. I took them for about two weeks and decided that I was not going to be a guinea pig for the government and I quit taking them. I would not take the shots either. My Lieutenant used to say he was a health-sciences major in college and that these vaccinations were good for us. I used to think he should have known better then and that is probably why he is in the Marines instead of working in the health care profession.

Around Christmas time, we moved to a location where the Army had set up a Hawk missile site. Our mission was to guard it. I remember thinking to myself, "Typical Army, they have all this shit and can't even guard it. It's probably better this way. If they got attacked they'd probably lose the Hawk missile site." Then, once we were settled in they gave us cots to sleep on. We were mad. We had been here since August, sleeping on the sand with all the scorpions and these guys were up on cots. "It figures", we thought.

Everyone used to get boxes in the mail with things we requested, mostly food items. We all used to put our food together and share it. We would make meals out of everything. Smoltz, Sven, Randal and myself used to share everything with each other. One day, right before Christmas, I got a box in the mail. It had a bunch of food in it. The best thing in it was the can of refried beans and tortilla chips. I rounded everyone up and we heated the can of beans on the engine block of the HMMV. There was also some peanut butter and crackers in the box. We all had a good meal with these items. It was so good in fact, that I was putting peanut butter on my last cracker and it fell into the sand, peanut butter side down. I was so angry. I decided to eat it anyways. I was not going to let this place take the one and only pleasure I had at Christmas time away from me.

A few days later, Smoltz received this giant circular tin in the mail. It was red and white and had Santa Clause all over it. I nick named it Smoltz's food blister. We all gathered around in anticipation as he opened it. Much to our liking, it was full of all kinds of delicious looking foods. We all cheered and Smoltz sneered at us.

"You guys can't have none. This is my Christmas present and I am eating it all."

"You little Mother-Fucker! You're going to share all of it. We shared everything with you."

Smoltz refused to share. So, when he was on guard duty later that afternoon, I devised a plan with Sven to get him back.

I dug a big hole in the sand. It was big enough for his food blister to fit in. The sand was level with the top of the lid. The container was about two feet tall. I did this so when he decided to pull the food blister out the lid would come off and all of the sand would fall in ruining all of his food.

I had decided that this was not going to be good enough. We were really mad at Smoltz for not sharing. I proceeded to dig a two-foot deep hole in front of the food blister and behind it. I placed thin pieces of cardboard from the MRE boxes over the holes. I then covered them up with sand. Then, Sven and I just laid there on our cots and waited for Smoltz to arrive.

Sure enough, a little while later, Smoltz returned. He came running back to us yelling, "Serocki, Sven we get to go to the PX and get smokes and sodas!" As soon as he said that he stepped right in front of his food blister and wham! He fell into the hole and racked his nuts. He screamed in pain and then realized that he was going to fall on his food blister so, as I had figured, he tried to step over it with his other leg to protect his precious food blister and wham! He stepped into the other hole and did the splits. Poor Smoltz was in serious pain. Sven and I were laughing so hard we nearly urinated all over ourselves.

We passed the sad days here by trying to make the place a little more like Christmas. I decorated my machine gun with some ribbons that were in my package from home. We made a Christmas tree out of a shovel handle and some of our old socks. Someone even got a game of risk in the mail. So, we used to sit in the back of a dump truck when we were not on guard duty and pass the time playing the game.

One day, after having returned from the PX back in Dhaharan, we started playing a game of risk. Someone had bought these cigarettes that were made out of leaves. They came all bundled together in a circular package. We each had taken one and lit up as we started the game. Next thing you know we all starting joking about how they smelled like marijuana. One thing led to another and we were all buzzed. We found out later that these were local cigarettes they made in Saudi Arabia and they contained some marijuana in them. As you can imagine these little cigarettes became a commodity. Finally, we had an escape!

At this Hawk missile site, I stood guard duty on top of this hill in a machine gun pit. Over the top of it was a cammie-net to hide us from the jets. We were closer to the Iraqi border now so the terrain changed a little. It was still mostly sand, but now it was a little hilly and the hills were usually somewhat rocky and harder than the surrounding soil.

I shared a fighting hole with a guy by the name of Zickowksi. He was Polish like me. So we got along pretty well. He now served as my assistant machine gunner. Muir had been transferred to a different platoon. One day Z-man, as I called him, received a cough syrup bottle in the mail. He called me over and told me to take a sip. I said,

"What for? I aint sick."

"Just fucking try it, trust me you'll like it."

So, I took a swig. Much to my enjoyment it was vodka. A good Polish drink! It was a small bottle, but we proceeded to drink it all and got a little buzz, which was nice.

One of the other things we started doing here to pass the time was to play football. We made up teams and had our own playoffs. In one game Z-man went to tackle Hart and got creamed. Because of our poor nutrition we were not at our strongest and Z-man broke his wrist that day. He got sent back to an aircraft carrier in the Gulf somewhere. He would remain there the rest of the war. He had to get screws put in his wrist. We all thought, "That lucky fucker. He gets a bed and good food and no one will try to kill him there. He found a ticket out of here."

We all had to figure out our own ways to help us deal with the situation we were all in. Sometimes we all did things together, like play football. However, most of the time you had to find ways to deal with your own mind. There was a war waging in front of us and one occurring in our minds. I often wrote home, telling my parents how I was trying to cope and about the wonderful things I had discovered about life.

December 6, 1990

Dear Mom,
I got a letter and a card from you today with a let-

ter from Amanda! Ya, Bush is kind of a peckerhead! That's the way it is with everything, they always pick the ones who don't have enough balls to question anybody point blank. When news people interview us they tell you what to say and to look happy. That's why you never seen me on the news, If I can't tell the truth then fuck'em. I'm not lying for the sake of our fearless president it's like being in Russia. I've had a couple of chances to get interviewed but I told the reporter to go to hell and I said "oh sure I tell you my story you go back to the states and change it to the way you want it and then put it on tv. Well fuck you pal!" And then I walked away and my lieutenant reamed me a new asshole and I told him, "for god sakes sir, I'm a human being not some robot you can program I don't need to be treated like this sir!" Well he told me to keep my mouth shut from now on. They asked me what I would say to the president I told them I would tell busch to shit or get off the pot! So that's probably why I didn't get picked, oh well! I hope Tom is doing better! Me and Bails are making a VCR tape and were using one tape so were gonna send it to his wife in California and she's gonna tape my part and send it to you so if you get a package from someone with the last name of Bails in California that's what it is. I don't know if it will make it for X-mas though. And you thought I wouldn't be home for the holidays didn't you! Well hopefully the tape will cheer you up. Hope so! Now mom, I want to tell you something I'm not trying to put you down, I'm trying to help you out here but I have to make you realize something first ok? So bear with me! I've been doing a lot of thinking over here. I realized most of my life I've been living in self pity for myself, always blaming everything on someone else. Well, I realized everything in my life is controlled by me! And my mind! So I made up my mind to quit living in self pity. So now everytime something bad happens I look at the positive things or side of it, there's always a positive side to everything! And I also started to count my blessings and I realized I am a very fortunate person. God created earth and said wow! Look at this beauty, so he created humans for no other purpose but to enjoy what he had created (nature). But so many people get caught up in work and self pitty and don't see the beauty god has created! All of my life I've listened to you and Tom complain how you never get to go out and your always working, no time for fun. Well that's your own fault! Your mind is a powerful tool! And depending on you it can make you wallow in self pitty all your life or have a great one! So this is what I want you to do! First you have to give this your all and actually try it! It will work trust me, It worked for me! Next time you start complaining about life, think to yourself, about everything good in your life! Like your husband who loves you, your three children, you have food on the table at every meal, you have nice house, two cars, a pool, and you've got yourself, you can walk, talk, run, think, see, hear, now I know if I can name all of those positive things in your life you can do it too! There are people in this world that don't have one of the things you do! So you see, you do have a great life! When something bad happens always look at the positive things don't look at the negative side or you will have a negative life and a negative out put to people and people now a days don't want to hear that stuff! So you know if I'm picking up those signals from you so are other people! Another thing have faith in god! He may only answer one of your prayers your whole life but some of gods best work is unanswered prayers. And everyday stop and smell the roses, notice the beauty god has created, not just one day a year but look every day! If you do all of these things your attitude and life will change dramatically but you have to try first. Like this morning I watched a bird in a tree for an hour. He was gray, black, and had white patches by his eyes. I watched him sharpen his beak on a branch and I listened to him sing and I watched him go through his daily routine and for a moment we looked at each other and I know we both wondered about each other and it was like the bird said goodbye to me and he gracefully flew away. And it put me in such a good mood today! See it works. Do this every morning when you get up, even if you stare at the same leaf everyday you'll notice something different about that leaf each time you look at it! And do you know who taught and helped me to think this way, through letters and books he sent to me out here, your brother, my uncle Dennis! He's a great guy mom, you should listen to what I have just told you and try it! He helped me a lot to be able to cope with things out here, positive thinking! Mom, remember that! Well it's time to go, take care and I love you all very much!

    Love,
    Robert

December 17, 1990

Dear Mom,
About my car just forget it for now ok. I've been

getting all of my packages. I don't have insurance on my car because of that bounced check, and I never had time to get it so ford sent me a letter saying I have to have insurance on my car and If I don't show proof of insurance they're gonna tack it on my payments. So they'll probably send me a new payment book. So have Tom call them (Ford Motor Credit). The ones you pay my car bill to and have him tell them what my situation is and see if he can't clear this mess up! Maybe he should give them your address so all the letters and stuff they send me goes to you cause I can't do nothing about that shit here! When I call you guys I switch off every time between you two when I go to the rear. Well I called dad and it was your turn to get a call next time I was in the rear, but there was no next time because we don't go to the rear no more because of the January 15th deadline so that's why you didn't get a phone call! I got Jerry's box it was nice. God I can't wait to come home, I'm so damn homesick I can't believe it! Who knows maybe I'll surprise you! Well take care mom!

Love ya lots,
Robert

December 19, 1990

Dear old Dad,

I've got a mission for you! One of my buddy's got a cough syrup bottle in his box from home and it was filled with VODKA! Well we each had a sip it was good! So what I want you to do is send about a pint of Bacardi 151 Rum. Send it in a shampoo bottle and put it in a box with some other shit and send it too me. If they find it I won't get in trouble the postal people will just get rid of it. Make sure you wash out the shampoo bottle or whatever you send it in good so we don't drink soap! Make sure you send a pint so there's enough for me, Smoltz, and Sven! Please send it fast! We are going crazy out here!

Love,
Robert

December 21, 1990

Dear Mom,
I got your letter yesterday. Things are ok I guess. They just told us about two minutes ago that a gas alarm went off at our Hawk missile site which we are next to so they said keep your gas mask next to you just in case. I hope it was just a drill. I think it was any ways. We went on a 6 mile hump yesterday and crawled through 800 meters of concertina wire for training. Well that's about it just another day in sand-nigger-land!

Take care,
Love,
Robert

December 22, 1990

Dear Dad,
Well, as for today I'm fucking pissed as hell and on top of that I have a cold and a cough, fuck what else is gonna happen? Well I'm pissed off because I came over here to fight a goddamn war, not to sit in this motherfucking desert for the rest of my life. So let's fight it and get the fuck home! I heard today that congress want's to vote to give the sanctions more time. Fuck the sanctions, lets kick the motherfuckers

ass NOW! Them fuckers in three piece suits sitting behind oak tables drinking spiced tea don't have the fucking right to make me sit over here in this fucking desert just so they can play their fucking political games! I'm not a fucking puppet goddamn it, lets do what we came here to do, now or go the fuck home. I don't feel like sitting in this motherfucker any more. I'm tired of the goddamned bullshit dad! Fuck am I pissed. Some old bald headed fucker playing games with my fucking life. What a bunch of cocks! I've got all this shit bottled up inside of me and they expect me to be happy and have moral. Well fuck them, let them assholes sit over here for 5 fucking months not knowing what the fuck is going on. Well you can tell what kind of day I'm having huh? Well I guess that's it dad. Take care.

Love,
Robert

December 25, 1990

Dear Mom,
How do you think I feel after watching "Born on the Fourth of July"? It hits home with me! I know what the poor guy is going through! The weather here is 80–90 degrees during the day and 35–45 degrees at night so I'm pretty much freezing my ass off! Don't get to intimate with this letter because I have a nasty cold right now! Yes I'm in a shit hole and I have a damn cold on Christmas, what else can happen? I suppose we could get attacked. Of course I probably wouldn't mind that. Ha ha ha. Shit I could never loose my sense of humor! Somebody has got to keep our moral up!

Amanda's teacher would have made a good expression but how did grandma and gramps take it? I really didn't want you to let them hear it because of the language on the tape but oh well! Well my Christmas sucked! I sat on a shitter last night freezing my ass off wondering what you guys were doing. Hope you had a good Christmas!
    Love,
    Robert

10

ONE

> *"I can't remember anything, I can't tell if this is true or a dream. Deep down inside I feel the strain. This terrible silence stops with me. I'm waking up I cannot see that there's not much left of me. Nothing is real, but pain now. Hold my breath as I wish for death. Oh please God, wake me! Darkness imprisoned in me. All that I see, absolute horror, I cannot live, I cannot die. Land mine has taken my sight, taken my speech, taken my hair and taken my arms, taken my legs, taken my soul, taken the LIFE in me."*
>
> By Metallica

While we sat in the sand waiting for the beginning of the ground war, the world moved on. Events were unfolding regarding the war and all of our lives. We however, were unaware of what was going on in the world that would decide our fate. We just sat and waited. The media wrote about the actions the President,

Saddam Hussein, and the world were taking relative to the debacle all of them had thrust us into.

The Arizona Republic
Sunday, January 13, 1991
Bush Handed War Power: Divided Congress backs president
By David Hess and R.A. Zaldivar
Knight-Ridder

After three days of impassioned debate, a deeply divided Congress voted Saturday to give President Bush the Power to make war on Iraq if it fails to withdraw from Kuwait by Tuesday. Bush said the vote "does not mean war is inevitable."

For most of us, the truly haunting question will be: How many young Americans will die?" Senate Majority Leader George Mitchell, D-Maine, said.

"For the families of those young Americans, the question will be: Did they die unnecessarily? No one will ever be able to answer that question. For if we go to war now, no one will ever know if sanctions would have worked, if given a full and fair chance."

Iraq facing blitzkrieg: War scenario outlined
By Mark Thompson
Knight-Ridder

If the Pentagon kept to its pledge to crush Iraq while protecting U.S. lives, the whine of war likely would begin after nightfall, when dozens of U.S. warships would launch hundreds of Tomahawk cruise missiles at key installations in Iraq and Kuwait.

From ships in the Persian Gulf and Red and

Tomahawks would streak at 55 mph toward targets deep inside Kuwait and Iraq. Their accuracy would put them through a football goal post at the end of an 800-mile flight.

Although the nation's war plans are among its most tightly held secrets, an emerging consensus among military experts both inside and out of the Pentagon concludes that any U.S.-led attack on Iraqi forces in and near Kuwait would begin with an unprecedented aerial bombardment that would "turn desert sand to glass," one Army officer said.

Bush says war is not inevitable: 'Rapid, massive withdrawal from Kuwait' needed
By Lyle Denniston
The Baltimore Sun

WASHINGTON- President Bush said Saturday that war is not inevitable but warned that fighting may begin "sooner rather than later" unless Iraq begins "a rapid, massive withdrawal from Kuwait."

With narrow but decisive majorities in Congress now backing military action if it is deemed necessary, Bush said a "critical moment in history" has arrived. He continued to stress that "peace is everyone's goal, peace is in everyone's prayers," but that is "for Iraq to decide."

Bush letter to Saddam released by Washington
The Associated Press

"The United States will not be separated from its coalition partners. Twelve Security council resolutions, 28 countries providing military units to enforce them, more than 100 governments complying with sanctions—all highlight the fact that it is not Iraq against the United States, but Iraq against the world.

That most Arab and Muslim countries are arrayed against you as well should reinforce what I am saying Iraq cannot, and will not, be able to hold on to Kuwait or exact a price for leaving."

'No blood for oil,' protests say worldwide
By Maud S. Beelman
The associated Press

In a scene reminiscent of the 1960's, hundreds of thousands of anti-war protesters filled the streets, parks and market squares of Europe on Saturday to urge the world not to go to war in the Persian Gulf.

"No blood for oil," proclaimed banners at more than 100 rallies in Germany.

As part of an international day of action coordinated with anti-war groups, protests against the military buildup in the gulf were held in Germany, Britain, France, Italy, Switzerland, Sweden and Norway, as well as in the United States and Canada.

People across the United States staged sit-ins, marches and fasts. Others quietly prayed for peace as Congress voted to give President Bush authority to wage war.

Protestors in Los Angeles occupied offices of a lawmaker who supports military action, 1000 people marched outside the Florida Capitol, 700 marched in Philadelphia and 11 Indianapolis residents fasted for peace. About 200 protesters demonstrated in a cold rain on the Capitol steps. More than 12,000 people showed up for a march in Portland, Ore.

One

Mom with son in Mideast, others set to go waits, prays
By David Cannella
The Arizona Republic

Mary Felts sits in the living room of her north Phoenix apartment and tries to keep track of the whereabouts of her nine grown children, five of whom have served in the military.

Two of her brothers served in Vietnam. She said one committed suicide while still in the Navy and the other returned after two tours in the Army and "has never been the same."

"He hasn't been able to hold a job," she said. "He drinks. He just has never been the same."

She said that they are a close family but, "we're all separated now."

"I pray there is no war."

War's environmental impact on gulf is debated
Reuters

LONDON-Raging fires, sunblotting clouds of smoke, massive oil spills and acid rain stretching to Pakistan could be some of the ecological battle scars of a war in the Persian Gulf, environmental scientists say.

John Cox, a chemical engineer and independent consultant associated with the party, said mines could set off fires burning 3 million barrels of oil from nearly 1,000 wells in Kuwait.

He predicted smoke could be as heavy as that from a nuclear explosion, blotting out the sun and causing temperatures in the region to drop as much as 15 to 45 degrees Fahrenheit during the day.

Most scientists gave more moderate forecasts.

John Pike, a climate specialist with the Federation of American Scientists, said from Washington a so-called nuclear winter would be unlikely.

"If all the wells went up simultaneously, it could create the kind of firestorm that would block out the sun, but it is very, very difficult to create those conditions."

Pike said it is more probable that smoke would shoot up and then come back down very quickly, bringing with it soot and the combination of sulphur dioxide and nitrogen oxide known as acid rain.

The long-term environmental impact of war is a relatively recent concern that arose along with the massive weapons of destruction developed in the past 40 years.

Saddam personifies war for GIs
Reuters

DHAHRAN, Saudi Arabia – Iraqi President Saddam Hussein has become a figure of myth and dream for many American soldiers in the Persian Gulf, their personalized hate figure as they steel themselves for a war that may start within days.

Pentagon officials said Thursday that U.S. forces would attempt to kill Saddam during an initial phase of a war.

But President Bush, asked at a press conference Wednesday whether Saddam was a target, refused to comment.

Most seem convinced that if Saddam is not ousted from power in Iraq, they will have to return to the gulf to fight him another time.

One

"He has to be stopped now before he goes any farther," said Army Spec. Robert Draus of Port Jefferson Station, N.Y. "We don't want to have to confront him four or five years from now when he's more powerful."

"We've been out here so long, we could kill Saddam Hussein for keeping us out here," Said Army Spec. Jeff Rinaldi of North Hollywood, Calif.

The day finally came when the war actually started. It was January 16th and we began flying sorties (bombing raids conducted by aircraft), literally hundreds of them a day. We had been awoken in the middle of the night by the ground shaking and loud noises. I got up and Corporal Haines was just peeking into our hole to tell Randal, Sven, Smoltz and myself that the air war had started just now. So we all peeked out from under the ponchos we had over our fighting hole and the whole horizon looked as if a thousand people were taking photographs with flash bulbs all over the place. Every time a bomb hit, the ground shook, sand fell in our hole, and the whole horizon lit up with exploding bombs and anti aircraft fire. This would continue for quite sometime, all night long and all day long. The only difference between night and day was that during the day you could not see the explosions because of the light.

We still moved around quite frequently, about every week to two weeks making new homes in the sand for ourselves, just like the bugs. One day we were all moving around out of our holes. We were conducting squad meetings and classes on how to call in air strikes and things like that. We were preparing to go into combat.

With our radios we would be able to get into contact with the pilots flying the jets when we called in for air support.

159

While we were going about our business we heard jets flying from the north towards our position. People started yelling "incoming!" We all scattered for our holes like hundreds of little ants before a rainstorm. We all dove into our holes under the cammie-netting in hopes we could hide from the jets. Then I listened. The planes flew in low and passed us by. As they passed by I heard this loud crack from the jet engines.

However, nothing happened. The jets just flew by. They must have been our planes. It was hard to tell whose jets were whose from a distance, with all the similar jets from all of the forces which belonged to the coalition we formed with the other countries. Besides, we did not have time to stand there and watch the jets to try and find out. Because if they were enemy jets and we were out in the open like that, we would become dead Marines.

I, as well as everyone else, hated digging these stupid holes all of the time. We would arrive at a new location, spend a day or two digging holes and fortifying our positions, and then it seemed like as soon as we were done with that we had to move again. I would get so angry. I always thought, "Can't we just stay still for a few days for crying out loud!" But, on this day I was never happier than I was at that moment to have dug a hole, when those jets flew overhead. I never complained about digging holes again.

As I mentioned before, Sven, Randal, Smoltz, and myself lived in a hole together. We had to dig a larger hole than the usual size to accommodate us all. The hole was usually dug under the cammie-netting next to an Amtrack. Once it was dug we buttoned our ponchos together and stretched it out over our hole and put sand and sand bags along the edges to hold it down so it would not blow away.

One

Then in the middle of the hole we would put a cammie-netting pole up under the poncho so we would have a peak in our makeshift roof.

One day, it started to rain on us. It just poured and it was cold. It was about fifty degrees or so. This was cold compared to the one hundred and thirty degree temperatures we had endured for so long. This is what winter is like in the desert. It rained for three days straight, non-stop. On the second night we were all sleeping and it was approximately a few hours until I had to be on guard duty. We had become used to the explosions and anti aircraft fire and an occasional scud missile flying over head to some unknown destination, much farther south than us.

We now slept right through these things. Then, while we were all sleeping the poncho had accumulated so much rain that it split in half and dumped what seemed like a few gallons of water all over us and our sleeping bags. We all woke up in shock. As soon as the shock wore off we all became extremely angry.

"Son of a bitch, the fucking ponchos caved in!"

"Fuck man I am soaking fucking wet!"

"All of our damn shit is fucking soaked, were soaked to the bone. Mother fucking cock sucker, what else is gonna happen next?"

We were all soaked, enraged, and now freezing to death. The wind was really howling.

"Who has the driest sleeping bag?"

"I think I do", I replied.

So all four of us got inside my sleeping bag and sat in the corner of our hole, which was the only place our poncho roof still stood. We stayed awake all night shivering. When daylight finally came, it was still raining and it continued to rain the whole day. We went about our business the next day.

We were all just completely soaked. The sand stuck to everything, the wind was blowing and it was damn cold. "What the fuck am I doing here?", I asked myself constantly. "I sure hope these fucking rag heads appreciate what we all are doing here because this sure the hell ain't no fucking vacation!"

A few days later Sergeant Martin came to my hole to talk to me.

"Hey, Serocki."

"Yeah, what's up Sergeant Martin?"

"We are going to get to go to the PX tomorrow and I want you to go"

"Alright."

"So get a list of things everybody in your squad needs and bring it with you. We will leave at 4:30 in the morning. Trent and Jones are going with us."

"Aye, aye Sergeant Martin."

So, I proceeded to compile my list of things that everyone needed and collected their money.

The next morning I got up at four in the morning. It was still dark out. I made myself some coffee and tried to wake up. I was so tired and so weak all the time. The bad food, no sleep, and battling the elements were taking their toll on me. The sun finally started to come up. I climbed out of my hole and set my jacket down in the sand. I went over and talked to Sergeant Martin and he said he was ready to go. So I went back to my hole and grabbed my jacket off of the ground and put it on. It was still cold and cloudy. I got into the HMMV and all four of us drove off into the desert. It would take us four hours to get to the big PX and base camp that was set up in Dhaharan. It was where all of our supplies were unloaded and then subsequently dispersed from there.

One

While we were driving my right upper trapezoid started itching. So, I scratched it, but it kept itching. I thought it was a tag scratching me. I stuck my hand under my jacket and shirt to rip the tag off and much to my surprise there was a shit beetle in there and it bit me.

"Son of a fucking bitch, you little mother fucker!"

"What's the matter Serocki?"

"Fucking goddamn shit beetle bit me on the fucking neck. I'm not gonna get hepatitis or anything am I?"

"I don't know for sure, but I doubt it."

So I pulled the shit beetle out and whipped it out the window into the desert. "Those damn fucking bugs, fuck those things piss me off!"

We finally made it to the PX. We bought all of our stuff. It was evening now and Sergeant Martin said,

"Lets all go make phone calls before we leave."

"Cool, lets go!"

So we all went to call home. Everyone was happy. We got to talk to family back in the real world. We escaped this desolate hellhole of a place for just a few minutes. It was so nice to be able to forget about everything else and not suffer for a little while, even if it was only for a few minutes. By the time we all got done and reassembled it was dark. We left and we would have to drive back to our position in the dark. This was going to be difficult because we could not use our headlights once we turned off into the desert from the highway. There also were no lights at our position.

We had finally turned off into the desert. We drove for quite some time and could not find our position. We then stopped and Sergeant Martin and I got out and stood on the hood of the HMMV in hopes we could see something, but we saw nothing. We listened for a while, but again, we heard nothing.

A Line In the Sand

"Well, lets keep driving north", Sergeant Martin said.

"We should run into one of our diversion units that have all their lights on and making all of that noise."

"Ok, lets go then", I said.

The Marines had set up some diversion units around the border to trick the Iraqi's into thinking we were somewhere that we were not. So we drove for a while. We soon came upon this little guard shack on the horizon with a light on.

"You see that Serocki?"

"Yeah."

"That must be the diversion unit I was talking to you about. When we get close I will stop the HMMV and you get out and go up to the guard and find out who it is and ask him if he can help us make our way back to camp."

"Aye, aye Sergeant Martin."

We pulled within twenty yards or so from the guard shack. I left my M60 machine gun in the HMMV. I got out of the vehicle with my pistol strapped to my hip. I started walking towards the guard shack, but I could not see who was there because the guard had a flash light and he was lowering it, raising it, and shining it in my eyes. As I got closer, I put my hand in front of my eyes to block the light and I said, "Who the fuck is this?" No one answered and the light kept shining in my face, moving up and down. I repeated what I said earlier, "Who the fuck is this damn it? Shut that fucking light off asshole, I'm a Marine." Then I got right up to the guy and I noticed a big red and white-checkered turban on his head and I immediately stopped breathing.

The Arabic man started yelling something in Arabic and I could not understand what he was saying. I looked down and saw the barrel of an AK47 nestled in my stomach. I had my hand on my pistol ready to pull it out. I thought, "If I pull it out chances are I will get shot first right in the gut." So I

One

kept my hand on my pistol and slowly backed up, still facing the Arabic man. He kept saying things in Arabic to me. When I got a safe distance away I turned and ran and I dove into the passenger seat of the HMMV.

"Get the fuck out of dodge now, get the fuck out of dodge now!"

"What the fuck is going on Serocki?"

"We just ran into an Iraqi camp, we are across the border. The guy had his gun in my gut." "Get the fuck outta here now!"

So Sergeant Martin quickly turned the HMMV around and floored it. I looked in the mirror and saw three sets of headlights following us in the distance.

"Holy fuck Sergeant Martin, they are following us in three vehicles."

"Alright Serocki, this is what we are gonna do. I am gonna pull over and we all will get out and you lock and load that M60 and get ready to rock and roll."

"Aye, aye Sergeant Martin."

We pulled over and I set my machine gun on the hood of the HMMV and locked and loaded it. My hands were shaking and my heart was pounding. I was nervous, but I did not have time to worry about anything. During situations like this, time seems to take on new meaning. It seems like it moves in slow motion, but then when its over it seemed like it lasted a millisecond. The adrenaline rush was exhilarating.

The vehicles approached and all four of us were ready. I tightly gripped my M60 and aimed in on the lead vehicle and all of a sudden they just sped right by us as if they did not even see us.

"Those dumb fuckers didn't even see us Sergeant Martin."

"Alright lets get in the vehicle and get outta here in case their buddies are coming."

So we drove for about a half hour and came across a Marine camp and the guard stopped us. "Where are you guys from?" We explained our situation and what had just happened. "Those three vehicles that just drove through here were Saudi's. They thought you guys were Iraqi's. They got scared and got the hell out of dodge."

We laughed. He told us about where we were and so we decided to drive off a little ways and stop for the rest of the night and finish our trip back in the morning when we could see better.

I could not sleep that night in the front seat of the truck. I would fall asleep and immediately wake up with my heart pounding a mile a minute and sweating profusely even though it was cold out. I was too scared to sleep. I was afraid someone would sneak up on us and kill us. My mind kept replaying the events of the night over and over again in my head. I kept panicking every time my mind did this. I kept thinking, "One false move and I would have been dead. All that guy had to do, was pull the trigger and I would have been Swiss cheese. I would have died and it would have been by the gun of a Saudi who was on our side.

"Holy shit," I thought. "God must really love me. I was so close to being killed and I wasn't, I was still alive to fight another day." I said a prayer and begged God to help me and keep me safe and I thanked him. I did the sign of the cross on my chest and I finally fell asleep. The next morning we found our camp and made it back all in one piece. I was never so glad to see my hole in the ground again.

A few days went by and things were back to normal during the day. At night the air raids continued and bombs exploded across the border lighting up the horizon every few seconds, as sand fell on us from the walls of our holes as

One

we tried to sleep. Then, one evening just after dark, someone spotted some cars heading our way through the desert. We were out in the middle of nowhere, quite a distance from the freeway. We suspected they were Iraqis, disguised as civilians, trying to find our location. Corporal Haines, who was our squad leader at the time, came running over to me and said,

"Get that machine gun ready. I am going to stop the car. If there is any trouble just shoot, don't worry about me. Do you understand?"

"Yes," I said.

"This is an order Serocki. If there is trouble I am ordering you to shoot at me. Got it!"

"Yes, Corporal Haines. I understand clearly."

So the car came slowly by, about twenty yards in front of my hole. It was a big Cadillac with a couple of Arabs inside. Corporal Haines stopped the car. I locked and loaded the machine gun and waited. Nothing happened. Haines questioned them and sent them on their way back. Haines told us they were a family, with kids, who apparently were lost.

Sometimes we would get stray cars and people out in the desert just trying to get the hell out of the country, but this time I thought they were Iraqi spies using kids as pawns in some sort of sick chess game thinking we would not kill them. Or maybe they thought we would hesitate and they would be able to kill us. Well, not a chance. I was prepared to do what I had to do to survive and win. Just like my drill instructor said, "If you hesitate at the moment of truth, you will become dead Marines and I did not give you permission to die!"

By this point in the war, I was so fed up with this place that I was willing to kill anything that lived, walked, crawled or breathed. I just did not care anymore and it just did not matter. All that was on my mind was killing the enemy, whoever it was, and getting back home.

Way out there in the desert, which to us was the middle of nowhere, we were approached by more than just the local residents and Iraqis. News reporters were vigilant in trying to find us and to get a story to sell to the American people so they could make a buck off of our suffering and even cost us our lives. But, it does not matter does it. After all money is money, right?

The problem was that if they had gotten to us they would have taken down some notes, taken them back to the rear and twisted them somehow to make it interesting so it would sell. Thus, giving an untrue and totally biased story to the American people, not to mention putting us and our location all over television so everyone including Saddam, would see it. Then all Saddam would have to do is point his missiles in the appropriate direction and we would be dead. But, I guess this did not cross the reporters' minds.

One day, way off on the horizon behind us we spotted dust coming up in the desert. This usually meant vehicles were approaching. We could see for miles. We often had the advantage however, because we were camouflaged and could not be seen until they got close. Some of us loaded into two HMMV's. The vehicles had weapons on them. One had a 50-caliber machine gun and the other had a Mark-19, which is an automatic grenade launcher.

We met the source of the dust out in the desert and stopped them. They were reporters. We told them they had to turn around and get the hell out of there. They gave us some line about how they have a right to get our story and we had to let them. We simply told them that they were in our world now and if they did not leave we would proceed to turn them into camel food. Of course they said we could not do that. However, we simply stated again, that they were in our world and there was no sheriff out here and they had ten seconds to disappear. Besides, who would know? They would just have been listed as missing. We were not about to give our position away and get killed just so they could make a mockery of our suffering in their newspapers in order to sell them for the almighty dollar. The reporters however, always found a way to get what they needed in order to print their stories.

The Arizona Republic
Thursday, January 31, 1991

Ground battle raging: 12 GIs die near Saudi town
Republic Wire Services

DHAHRAN, Saudi Arabia – Iraqi troops and tanks thrust into Saudi Arabia from occupied Kuwait late Tuesday, seized a deserted town and fought allied forces in the biggest ground battle of the Persian Gulf War, an engagement that killed 12 U.S. Marines and possibly hundreds of Iraqis.

By early Wednesday, all but one Iraqi unit that had seized the town of Khafji had been forced to retreat into Kuwait, suffering heavy losses both to soldiers and equipment, Saudi and U.S. military sources said.

Saudi-led allied forces that tried to recapture Khafji on Wednesday night were driven back by the remaining Iraqi forces, which were estimated at 50 to 150 soldiers.

Some light-armored Saudi forces made it to the center of the town, but other allied forces, including U.S. Marines, were forced into a feverish retreat when pelted by Iraqi rocket fire just south of the town.

Retreating allied units later regrouped and apparently mounted a second assault on the town early today.

Allied military sources said Iraqi forces were massing on the Kuwaiti-Saudi border Wednesday night, possibly heralding further forays into Saudi Arabia.

Iraqi radio, proclaiming a major victory, said Iraqi President Saddam Hussein personally planned the attack.

The fighting, which erupted after four border probes by Iraqi units, was described as "hellacious" by one Marine.

Finally, war gets real for Marines
By John Balzar
Los Angeles Times

EASTERN SAUDI ARABIA – It no longer was an enemy off in the distant dunes, lobbing occasional artillery shells. It no longer was a high-altitude Nintendo war.

When illumination flares popped over the cold desert late Tuesday, U.S. Marines looked down the 30-foot long cannon barrels of advancing Iraqi tanks and heard the roar of guns.

For the Marines positioned near the border town of Khafji, the opening moment of the great ground war was upon them.

Never mind later assessments that this was only an Iraqi reconnaissance in force, a challenge, a probe, an attempt to lure U.S. forces into Kuwait. For these first hours, the tanks and vaunted battle-hardened army of Iraqi President Saddam Hussein bore

One

down, and the 1st and 2nd Marine divisions were locked in the kind of close-in combat that is the specialty, the glory, of the corps.

TOW missiles, the wire-guided tank killers, exploded from light-armored vehicles in the Marine positions.

It was now January 30, 1991, my 21st birthday. What a place to be on such a landmark in a young persons life. It was like the joke we had for the letters U.S.M.C. We said it stood for, "U Signed the Mother-fucking Contract!" That is the first thought that popped into my head that day.

Later on that afternoon, a vehicle showed up. It was one of ours. Sergeant Martin unloaded a box off of it and carried it over to where we all were. He told me to take a seat on the hood of the HMMV. So, I did. He had a case of warm Pabst Blue Ribbon near beer. Then Sven shows up with a chocolate nut cake out of an MRE. He stuck a piece of paper in it and lit it on fire. The whole platoon sang me happy birthday. It was funny. I laughed. Everyone got one near beer and I got two because of my birthday. We drank the warm near beer and made plans of how we would celebrate this momentous occasion back in the real world when we got home.

All of a sudden a call came over the radio, "Tear down your nets, tear down your nets!" We started scrambling to tear down our cammie-netting. We finally found out that at least forty Iraqi tanks had crossed the border and rolled into the town of Khafji. We had orders to go join the battle. I thought, "This fucking day just keeps getting better and better."

We got packed in a hurry and loaded into the Amtracks. We got within several miles of the town. We received orders to wait until the grunts called us in to get them out of a jam.

A Line In the Sand

They were fighting from building to building. The Egyptians and Saudi's were also helping out, if that's what you want to call it. Everyone was mixed together in the town, including the enemy. There was no battle line. We were listening on the radio and watching from where we were. Things started to get pretty bad. The grunts were fiercely fighting, but things were getting crazy with the tanks. The Marines then called in an air strike on their own position. There was no other way out. There was no enemy or friendly side.

The next thing you know we were all taking cover and watching, unable to help our fellow Marines, as the A-10 Warthog jets came in for an air strike. They started dropping rockeye all over the place. Rockeye are large canisters that look like bombs, but when they get about two hundred feet above the deck (the ground) they split open. Once they split open one thousand little rockets come flying out in all directions. They go through anything, even tanks and especially people.

They were dropping what seemed like a hundred of these canisters. All of sudden they were all splitting open and it sounded like thousands of arrows flying through the air. Then, things started exploding all over the place and all kinds of things were flying through the air. It looked like a thousand sparklers went off amidst a cloud of smoke. It all lasted for only a few minutes, but it seemed like an eternity. We then got the call to go in and kill any enemy that was still alive and to take a count of our dead bodies.

So, we went into Khafji looking for dead bodies. There was smoke all over the place, some fires still burning. The smell of burnt flesh and hair was thick in the air. The smell was nauseating. To this day, the memory of that smell makes me want to vomit. I approached an LAV, which looks like a tank with four tires. I opened the back hatch and

One

peered inside. What was left of the Marines that were in there was reduced to a puddle of slop at the bottom. There were small pieces of unidentifiable flesh sticking to the sides and floor of the vehicle. They were burnt and melted. They were stuck in position by an adhesive of blood. I could not even find any dog tags. Everything had just melted. I could not tell how many Marines were in the vehicle when it got hit.

The LAV was riddled with holes from the little rockets. It looked like Swiss cheese. The light from outside was shining through the holes and it highlighted the dust particles suspended in the air. The glass in the turret is about four inches thick and it was completely melted. It was hanging down from the turret like icicles. I quickly closed the door and walked away. I began to heave. Nothing came out. I had nothing in my stomach to vomit.

This was how everything looked. Everything was burnt, full of holes and dead. Buildings were blown to pieces. Humans were blown to pieces. Their war torn bodies still smoking. The town was no more. What once was loud, noisy and chaotic is now quiet, desolate and still. The place was frozen still by death. "Wow, what a fucking 21st birthday", I thought. "I will never forget this day as long as I live." We found no one alive and could not really assemble an accurate count of the dead. Most of their bodies were reduced to ashes, pieces and goop. You could not tell what pieces belonged to what pieces. Some of the grunts who were here did live. But, I only heard this. I never knew who it was or even saw them. We loaded back into our vehicles and went back to the position we came from and awaited our next orders.

At this same location, which seemed to be popular with visitors, we had other even more un-welcomed guests than the previous ones. They are otherwise known as rats. For a place that has no plants and no water anywhere to be seen, these sure were big "fucking rats." They were the size of a full grown male's foot! They were everywhere. They only came out at night, which made it worse. The nighttime was already scary enough, but now we had to worry about something else.

They would come out into our holes at night. You would be laying in your sleeping bag and these big nasty rats would crawl across your sleeping bag every few seconds. They would crawl over your feet, legs, arms and even your face. It was disgusting.

One day we got a case of Pepsi delivered to us. So, after we drank the Pepsi I gathered everybody's cans and told them I had a plan to catch the rats. I cut off the tops of all the cans and put crumbled up crackers from the MRE's in them. I made trails to the cans with creamer. When it got dark Sven and I took first watch, both armed with shovels. We always stood guard duty together even though it meant a double shift for us. We did it because he was my assistant machine gunner now and he was no good to me asleep if we got attacked and as I stated before, the nighttime was scary. I hated the night. You could not see a damn thing. You felt like a sitting duck.

As we sat there quietly, we started to hear cans rustling. We went over to the one that was moving and this rat got his head stuck in the can. The thing was so damn big and fat that it could only fit its head into the Pepsi can. We then proceeded to smash the rats head flat! Once we did that, we took it back into our hole and everyone in the squad followed us. We had a poncho over the top of the hole like a roof. We went into the corner, which was shaped like a "U". We turned on this flashlight with a red lens and looked at

One

the rat. Sven had the rat by the tail. As it was dangling and we were admiring our handy work, we noticed that there were thousands of mites crawling out of the rear end of the rat. We all screamed and we were fighting each other to get out of the hole.

Sergeant Martin came running over to see what all the commotion was and we got in trouble for making noise at night and he sent everybody back to bed. Sven and I finished our watch.

The next morning when we got up we noticed Corporal Morris and Smoltz were missing from their holes, which were out on the perimeter away from the main camp. We put all of our holes out about one hundred yards due to the fact we were carrying a few thousand pounds of explosives with us.

We thought Morris and Smoltz had been captured or even killed. However, we found them back at base camp sleeping on top of the Line Charge trailer. This was a big trailer that contained seventeen hundred and fifty pounds of C-4 explosives. It looked like a big box that contained a long rope of sausage links that were the size of beer cans and it was shot off of an arm out into a minefield and detonated. The explosion would detonate all the mines and we would then send a mine plow through the area, which is a tank with a big bulldozer blade on it. After that everyone could then proceed through the minefield.

Sergeant Martin found those two and chewed them out. I thought he was going to beat them. He gave them a speech about abandoning their post and abandoning all the rest of us. He then proceeded to tell them that they would stand all the guard duty for the next week, all night long and during the day they would have to dig a hole with e-tools big enough to fit the line charge trailer in. The trailer was about the size of an SUV. He made them do it.

When we got back to our holes Sergeant Martin called me over. Somehow I got dubbed as the platoons rat killer. This was my new mission for the time being. He had a rat tunnel that went all around his hole and it went up to the surface, and the rat was still in it. Sergeant Martin gave me an order to kill the "mother-fucking rat", as he put it. I grabbed his bayonet and told everyone to back away. I put the bayonet in my mouth and jumped into the hole. I proceeded to stab at the rat. He ran back and forth dodging my bayonet thrusts. You see these rats were also very agile. Finally, I pierced the rat through his gut. Blood squirted out and bubbled on the bayonet blade. I stood up and held the rat over my head and screamed, "Mission accomplished Sergeant Martin." Everyone laughed.

Amidst all this excitement, which was almost too much to bear, I was still receiving tapes from my dad on a frequent basis. They became a source of entertainment for all of us. Every time I got a tape I would let everyone know and they would all gather around in my hole and listen. My dad was hilarious on the tapes. He would get pissed off at the news media and Saddam and start screaming, yelling and cussing. Everyone would get a good laugh out of it and they all would say, "You should get your dad to come out here and kick some ass."

One day while Sven and I were stuck in our hole because of a major sand storm, we decided to make a tape summarizing everything that happened to us up until this point. We wrote out a script and we each took turns reading it onto the tape. Then, after we spoke we would play a song or two that related to what we were talking about. We

One

were going to try and continue it throughout the war, but we never did. We got separated shortly after that and at that point the war heated up. However, I kept the tape. After these events had occurred, I wrote home to my family to let them know what was going on.

January 3, 1991

Dear Mom, Tom and Amanda
I got a letter from you yesterday, well actually it was a card. It's 27 more days until my 21st birthday. I'll probably kill a few ragheads on that day to compensate for me being here on that day! Right now we are having a massive sandstorm I can barely right this damn letter because I can't open my eyes barely and it's hard to write with a layer of sand on my paper! Well, take care!
Love ya,
Robert

January 11, 1991

Dear Mom, Tom and Amanda,
Hey mom you notice whose name I always put first on your letters, yours! So Theresa and Liz got a kick out of my letter huh. Are they going to write me back? I don't mind getting a little extra mail. I don't know how much leave I'll get I'm really not worried about that , I'm just concentrating on making it out of this motherfucker alive, oops sorry about that word but that's what we call this place! Well right now we moved up to the border into our attack positions and we dug trenches, fighting holes and giant holes to sleep in. So I'm back to sleeping in a hole and on top of that it's been cold as hell and it's been raining so our holes

filled up with water, my sleeping bag is drenched, my clothes are soaked and the wind is blowing and basically I'm freezing my ass off!!!! Let me put it this way mom we are going to war unless by some very slim chance Saddam pulls out between now and the next 4 days. Tell Pat and Ceil I got there box it was great thanx. I can't write them back because I lost there address off the box. I feel bad so call them and tell them I said thanx! I love you guys a lot!!! Take care.

Love,
Robert

January 15, 1991

Dear Dad,

I have included a roll of film, don't bother sending me the doubles because I'll be in combat by then. Brian wanted some pictures to show his buddies so give him the doubles if you want. This may be the last letter you receive from me because I doubt I'll have a chance to write once I'm in combat keep writing me just in case we get mail. We are on yellow alert because they are expecting an air attack by the Iraqi's on us within 48 hours we are all getting nervous. Everybody is wondering if they are gonna get shot or make it home in one piece. I'm pretty scared dad. I just want to tell you that I love you very much and I can't wait to come home. Be strong for me and the rest of the family dad. I guess it's time to do my job. I love you dad! Take care!

Love ya lots,
Robert

February 6, 1991

Dear Mom,
Well, shit I don't even know what the hell to write.

One

I don't know what to say any more. I'm so fucking pissed off!! They should just drop some low intensity nukes on the asshole and end it all!! So I can come home. This Iraqi captain we captured said that if somebody would just kill Saddam this would all be over with. Well why don't those cocksuckers do it ya know? I'm so sick of being dirty, hungry, cold, wet, hotter than hell, bored, tired, scared, and wondering, wondering when I'll come home? What will happen to me? Will I get shot? Will I live, or will I die? When the hell are we gonna do what we gotta do? I wish some one would answer these questions for me. I got a card from you today that you sent on January 25th, thanx. It was nice. God I want to come home. It just seems like this will never end sometimes. I keep trying to fool myself by saying, "this will be over soon, it can't last to much longer." But I can't fool myself because I know that I don't have any hard core evidence that that's what will happen. So what am I supposed to think now? Hope you guys are alright. Other than that I'm fine. You guys take care and I miss you all very much!!

Love ya lots,
Robert

February 7, 1991

Dear Dad,

How about going to work eh! I'm fine. Don't worry dad, tell Dan and Mike this, we are kicking some arab ass!! In two or three days they are supposed to drop some 15,000 pound bombs on them cocksuckers. We saw the scuds go right over our heads and get blown up. I get scared a lot nowadays. We are not in Khafji but we are in artillery range.

They tell us every day that we've got to swallow fear and shit intimidation. Yeah we have to watch out and take care of each other that's the only way we can all make it through this alive. Have you ever seen one of your best buddy's die in front of your face or have to patch him up when he gets wounded? I don't like that shit but I do it. One thing you have to understand dad and prepare your self for. When I come home the war will be over for you, but not for me. It'll always be there in the back of my mind haunting me. Your gonna have to bare with me when I get home. It's gonna be rough on me. Well dad I'm fine so you take care and I love you too!!
    Love,
    Robert

February 11, 1991

Dear Dad and Steph,
Well it's another day less I have to spend here! Fuck I wonder how many more I've got to go? It seems like a fucking eternity ya know. During the day I can hear and feel the bombs. But at night I can see the explosions, hear them, and feel them!! The horizon is nothing but one big fireball and black smoke! I can see the planes shooting missiles at the enemy and see where they explode! I can also see the enemy shooting anti-aircraft guns at the planes and I can see them shooting orange and green flares into the air! Sometimes I can see missles and shit fly over my head at night! There's never a fucking peaceful moment around here no more. I can see and hear hundreds of jets and B-52's flying over my head! It's pretty scary but it happens so often and is so much a part of my life and everybody elses now

One

that we're getting used to it. At first everybody would hit the deck when we heard or saw the shit, then people would just start ducking and flinching at the shit. Now we all just stand outside watching saying, "holy fuck, did you see that one? Some sorry son of a bitch just got fucking slaughtered, cool!" In fact bombs are going off now as I am writing this letter and sand and rocks are falling off the walls of my foxhole on me. And I'm just sitting here writing you like nothing's going on. Am I crazy? What's happening to me dad? I feel so different. At times I feel like a little child and at other times I feel like an old man. We just moved again, I'm sure you can tell which direction we moved in by the description I just gave you. I've dug a new hole. I got knee deep and hit solid rock and then I had to use the pick and brake the rock up and shovel it out until I got the hole waist deep. It took me a day and a half to dig the motherfucker, non stop digging, what a bitch!!! Now to top everything off I'm dirty as fuck, my armpits smell like onion fields, my hair is gray from all the dust, I have a pound of sand and rock in my sleeping bag not to mention the rocks I sleep on. And the best part about it all is I got little friends that sleep with me. They're called rats! Yeah, rats, big fuckers with dicks this big——— ha ha ha. Last night I had one crawl on my face and he decided to stop and take a rest and I woke up and smacked him to the other side of the hole. He hit the wall then the ground, recovered and hauled ass. God I love this fucking country, yeah right! And now to top it off it's cold as fuck! This morning I woke up and there was frost all over everything that's fucking cold man!! But other than that I'm doing fine and I CANT WAIT TILL THIS SHIT IS OVER! And I can come

home, fuck it seems like I'll be here forever. Well take care, I love you guys a lot!!!!!!!!
Love,
Robert

Here are two letters, which I still had. They were written to me, by my father and sister. I had been saving their letters all along, however when the battle of Khafji happened, we were instructed to burn all of our letters or anything with addresses on it. Our superiors were worried that an Iraqi would find the letters with the addresses and send a letter bomb home to our parents.

January 30, 1991, 1 a.m.

Hi Robert,
How are ya? I guess 12 marines got killed and it really shook me up! Bad! It must be scary where your at. I hope everyone looks out for each other. I'm sure they do. Happy Birthday. I wish you could spend it in the states with us. I feel sorry for you! I will write your friend. Well, take care of yourself!! Love ya lots and lots!!! Miss ya lots! I can't wait to see you again!
Love ya! Steph

Wednesday January 30, 1991, 8 p.m.

Hi Robert,
Happy birthday, nice way to spend your 21st birthday. Like I said before we will take care of that when you get home. I received your letter today that you wrote on the 15th of January. Today 12 marines were killed and 2 wounded. What division are you with? Is the unit a light armor division? Is the unit the infantry what number if it is? I guess I want to know

One

because I have good map and I'm trying to keep track of you. Can you tell me what town your near? If not are you west of Khafji (the town that Iraq got into on January 29 near the Kuwait border). How far 100, 50, 25 miles? By the time you get this letter you will have moved many times. They showed what they are doing to the Iraq army and country. It's really knocking the shit out of them. I would rather have you in back somewhat. It's just as good as going in at the middle or tail end then first. That's when most of the people get hurt. You and I still have a lot to do yet when you get back. Its 5 am where your at. Can you see the bombs hit or hear the noise? Could you hear the scud missiles or see them when they fired them at Saudi Arabia? Well if you get a chance to write drop a line. Love you miss you and cant wait to see you.

Love Dad,
OXOX
P.S. Take care and watch out for each other. We can't send any more packages to you.

February 19, 1991

Dear Dad and Steph,

I've been getting your mail and everyone else's. I've been picked for a secret mission. I'm not with 1/7 anymore. I'm still with an infantry unit. It's called RCT4 (regimental Combat Team #4). I can't tell you anything else. Call everyone and tell them I'm doing fine and that I probably won't be writing any more. Tell them to keep writing me though. Call Lonnie and Terry and Johnny and tell them all of the above. They told us that the war shouldn't last much more than a week once the ground troops go in. Then they said they are already making arrangements for us to fly home as soon as the

A Line In the Sand

shit is over with. They said the first ones in will be the first ones out and we were one of the first units over here. So it looks like it'll be all over with soon dad. So you and Steffy hang in there, ok! Don't worry I'll be ok, because I'm one bad motherfucker!! And only the good dye young and I'm one hell of an asshole so it looks like I'll be coming home alive pops!!!! Can you believe it dad, your son got picked for a secret mission!!! Boy I'm gonna be one hell of a war hero—eh? You'd be proud as hell of me if you only know what I was about to do! I'll tell you all about it when I get home!!! It'll be soon guy's! I love you and miss you guys a lot and you guys mean the world to me!!! Make sure you tell mom that also for me ok? I'll kick some serious ass for you guys. Take care, and I love ya lots!!!!!!!

Love ya,
Robert
P.S. See ya soon!!!

11
EVE OF DESTRUCTION

The eastern world it is exploding. Violence flaring, bullets loading. Your old enough to kill, but not for voting. You don't believe in war, but what's that gun your toting. And even the Jordan River has bodies floating, but you tell me over and over and over again my friend how ya don't believe we're on the eve of destruction. Don't you understand what I'm trying to say? Can't you feel the fears I'm feeling today? If the button is pushed there's no running away. There will be no one to save with the world in a grave. Take a look around you boy. It's bound to scare ya boy. And you tell me over and over and over again my friend how you don't believe we're on the eve of destruction!

By Barry McGuire

We had been gearing up for the ground war now for about a month. We moved north closer to the Kuwait border. We were told we were about eight miles from it.

Sometime in February my platoon Sergeant, Sergeant Martin, came to me and told me I had been picked for a special mission. It was about two weeks before the ground war was actually supposed to start. He said, "I picked you Serocki, because I know you know your shit." I said, "Ok, no problem." A few days had passed and Randal and I were packing our gear to leave to form the new unit. I gave my M-60 machine gun to Sven and took his M-16A2 rifle. He wanted the nine-millimeter pistol I had, but I said, "No fucking way man, this is the Captains and he told me to hang on to it and give it back to him when the war was over".

As I was getting ready to go Sergeant Martin came over to me. He was the perfect Marine, by the book, as hard as nails. I always looked up to him. He was like a dad to me. When he came up to me he said, "See ya later Robert". My heart stopped beating and fell to my stomach. He broke Marine Corps policy and called me by my first name. I knew now that I was in for a world of shit. I said, "See ya when it's over Ron, write my sister and tell her what happened". It was like we both understood each other. Like he knew I was thinking tell my sister I died heroically on a secret mission and I knew he was saying I picked you because if anyone could make it and enhance the success of the mission it would be you. He said he would and I piled on the truck with Randal and we drove off into the horizon.

At this point I did not think I would be coming home. Before I got picked for this mission, we were told that ninety percent of us would be dead in the first wave. I ignored it and just told myself that would not happen to me, besides I had already accepted death. However, now I really thought this was it. I started to think I had been picked for a suicide mission and I would not even have a chance to be in the ten percent that would make it.

Eve of Destruction

When everyone got to the assembly area we formed our new platoon. There were guys from different engineer units, a lot of them I did not know. Here I was, on the verge of going into combat and I did not know most of the people with whom I would be fighting. We were then attached to 2/7 and 3/7 (second and third Marines, seventh division), who were all part of task force Grizzly.

We soon found out what our mission was. We were tasked with a nighttime infiltration of two enemy mine fields, in which the enemy was dug in on the other side. Then we were to lead the grunts through it and clear and destroy the bunker complex the Iraqis inhabited. I thought to myself, "Holy shit, I am fucked". We would depart in about a week or so.

We would spend the next week training day and night to prepare for this mission. I was bound and determined to make it home, but it seemed as though we were up against such unwinnable odds that my dream of going home appeared to be hopeless. There was only going to be around fifty of us armed with M-16A2 service rifles against several thousand Iraqis with rifles, machine guns, mortars, artillery, tanks, and worst of all, chemical warfare. That is the Marine Corps though. They put you in a bad situation and expect you to win, no exceptions. Mission completion always comes first no matter what the cost.

Us engineers were supposed to infiltrate this minefield in a series of steps over a four-night period. I thought, "How the hell are we gonna crawl through a mine field to the door step of the enemy in one night without being caught, let alone on four nights!" We were to crawl through the minefield in a single row. On the first night we were supposed to locate all of the land mines in a path with a plastic stick. The old proven method was with a bayonet, but the enemy had metallic mines. If anything metallic touched them they would explode.

Once we located the mines we would then put three plastic spoons in front of the mine. One spoon would get placed in the middle and two on the ends. We were to do this all the way to the Iraqi bunker complex with all the Iraqis in it, looking for us. That would complete the first stage and we would have to then turn around keeping our single file row, and crawl back out before morning. Talk about intense stress!

The next night we were supposed to re-enter the minefield and string com-wire (a thin black wire used to hook up telephones, etc.) through the path we would have made the night before. Then, on the third night we were to take chemlights and put them in these special tubes, which would only show a tiny spot of light on the friendly side (towards us). After doing this we were to place these chemlights on the outer boundaries of the path we had been creating the past couple nights. Finally, on the last night we were supposed to lead the grunts through the minefield and eradicate the enemy on the other side.

This was our initial mission for the time being. However, in the Marines, a Marine knows that inevitably plans will change at least twelve times at the last minute. Finally, our day of reckoning came and we would finally get to cross the infamous "line in the sand" between Saudi Arabia and Kuwait.

That evening we crossed the border and the famous Iraqi ditch that they had constructed. We got to the other side and the area was littered with burnt out shells of Iraqi tanks and burnt, very dead, bloated bodies of Iraqi soldiers. It looked as if everything had been frozen in time by fire. I thought to myself, "I would be seeing a lot more of this under a lot worse circumstances." And, to top it off, my fellow Marines and I would be the cause of it. We would be the cause of total destruction of human lives. However, it did not bother me because I was so perturbed at the Iraqis for what they did to their fellow man, women and children. I was also incensed at them for making me come to this place of pain, suffering and death. There was nothing good about this place. They had been fighting since the time of Christ. Would I be able to change hundreds of years of violence and oppression? I did not know, but I had a mission to do and I would accomplish it whether I had to give my life to make it successful or not!

We finally made it to our forward assembly area. There was a large olive drab canvass tent, which was the command post. Inside there were radios and other communications equipment with several Marines inside manning the equipment. At this point we were with a grunt unit. I was not sure if it was 2/7 or 3/7.

We were all busy getting prepared for our mission. My unit was busy putting silver duct tape on each persons' back so that when the shooting started and people started crossing enemy lines in the dark through the minefields we would be able to tell who was who. While we were doing all of this I heard something soaring through the sky. It sounded kind of like a jet engine, but not quite as loud. Then, all of sudden, about twenty-five yards in front of our perimeter, there was an explosion.

The Iraqis were shooting at us with artillery. We could not even shoot back. You could not see who was shooting at you. A couple seconds later, another shell slammed into the earth, only closer. Every one started scrambling around frantically like ants right before a big storm. The Lieutenant started yelling, "Spread out, spread the fuck out!" So we did. I sat down in the sand and leaned against my pack, gripping my rifle. I said to myself, as the artillery shells were still coming in, closer and closer each time, "This is it Serocki, you are really in for it now." The shells would pound themselves deep into the ground as if someone was slamming them in with a giant hammer. Sand would fly and the ground would shake vociferously as the shells exploded and emaciated the soil, equipment and the humans near their tentacles of death. People were screaming and yelling, running this way and that way like they were marbles in a box whose sides were being lifted up and down and being turned left and right.

Just then, another shell found its way to the center of our perimeter. It penetrated the sand, the ground shook and the shell obliterated our command post. The next thing I saw was a HMMV pull up and a few Marines started tossing bodies of guys I had just seen and even talked to five minutes ago, in the back of the vehicle like sacks of potatoes. Once, the back filled up they started laying them across the hood. The HMMV was filled with lifeless bodies. I remember one guy in particular, which they placed on the hood. He had a large white pad on his chest. They put him on the hood and he was just lying there, not moving. It did not even look like he was breathing. "Man", I said, "I guess when it's your time, it's your time, you have no control over it. I could have been next to that tent, or even close to it, but I was not. What if the shell had just veered to the right a little bit? That would be me on the hood of that HMMV." I guess I was just lucky.

At that point, the artillery fire stopped. I did not know why, it just did. We all got back together and made sure we still had all of our people accounted for and no one was hurt. We settled into formation and prepared to head out into the darkness of the desert night in search of the Iraqi Army and cram death down their throats.

Once it became completely dark we headed out like vampires in search of a long overdue cocktail of blood. There were about fifty of us. There were twenty engineers and thirty snipers. We had one radioman, our Lieutenant, and the sniper's Staff Sergeant. We were all armed with M-16A2 rifles. We had been walking through the desert for quite some time. The desert was as flat as plywood here with no plant life. The ground was hard, like concrete, unlike the rolling hills of sand in Saudi Arabia.

There was not supposed to be any air strikes within two thousand meters of us (approximately the size of two city blocks). It was still about four days before the ground war was actually supposed to start and our flyboys were really peppering the border. They stepped up their bombing missions in preparation for the ground war.

While we were walking, we heard this loud crack in the sky. We all looked up in amazement as three jets flew over our heads. They were so close to us you could almost jump up and touch them as they went by. This low status of the jets could only mean one thing...they were coming in for a bombing run.

Our code name was Batman and headquarters was Bat Cave. All of a sudden the Staff Sergeant gets on the radio and starts yelling,

"Bat cave, Bat Cave, this is Batman, over?"

"Go ahead Batman, this is Bat Cave."

"What the fuck is going on? We just had three jets fly directly over our heads, over!"

"Di di mow, get the fuck out of dodge Batman. Those jets are coming in for a bombing run and they are dropping FAE bombs."

FAE stands for Fuel to Air Explosive. Our jets would drop fuel over the Iraqi positions and ignite it creating a horren-

191

dous explosion of fire. This explosion of fire would completely fry everything in its path and remove all of the oxygen in the air to fuel its fury. These bombs would wipe out a thousand meter area (the size of a grid square on a topographic map, which is approximately the size of an entire city block).

The Staff Sergeant turned to us and said, "Get the fuck outa here now!" We all started running as fast as we could through the desert. All I could hear was my breathing and my heart pounding so hard that I thought it would pop out of my chest. It was just like that time I was running for a touchdown when I played for the Bills, when I was a child. Only, my cousins were not on the sidelines dressed as cheerleaders screaming with enthusiasm for me.

While we were running I was looking at the ground and I saw a big land mine lying there. It was right in my path. I was running so fast that I did not have time to change directions. I just closed my eyes and took as long of a step as I could and hoped for the best. I got lucky and missed it. I yelled to the guys behind me to watch out for it and we kept on running.

Then, all of a sudden, it was like daylight in the middle of the night. We all stopped and turned around and looked at the horizon. It was now completely engulfed in a huge, orange fireball. Then there was a loud crack and I felt my clothes jump as if someone was trying to rip them off of me while I was still wearing them. The next thing I knew we were all on the ground saying, "Holy fucking shit!"

We were all ok. It felt like I was waking up with a hangover. We gathered our senses and headed back to camp. We would try again the next night. "Hopefully, the big cheeses back at battalion would not order any more air strikes in our area of operation." I was outraged. "They had to know we were there. They are the ones that planned this damn thing. Why would they call an air strike on their own people when it was not even necessary? Or maybe the flyboys could not read their radar?"

Then I thought, "Wow, I have gotten really lucky three times today and haven't even gotten a scratch. I have been shot at by cannons, almost stepped on a land mine, and last but not least, almost blown back to the cave man days by our own people." I hoped my luck would continue for the rest of the war. However, I began to worry that my luck would run out sooner or later. So, when we finally got back to camp and I crawled back into my hole, which resembled a grave, I said my prayers! I was going to do everything I could to make sure the odds were in my favor.

Here I was twenty-one years old, carrying guns and ammo, heading off to shoot people, lying down in a hole in the ground praying to God and getting wrapped up in superstitions. I had to have hope. I had to have some way to let myself know that I had some control over what would happen to me, that it was not up to someone else whether I lived through this war or not. If I did not pray and have faith in God, I surely would have gone crazy. God was giving me hope and confidence and I would do what ever it took to maintain that, no matter how silly and childish it seemed. I finally drifted off to sleep.

They next day when we awoke we began preparing for the next night's activities. This time the grunts would go on ahead and the engineers would come up behind a little later. We also found out that the government had some new equipment they wanted us to try out. We were given three backpacks, which weighed about one hundred pounds each. They were filled with C4 (a plastic explosive).

We were supposed to get to the edge of the minefield, set these things up and the C4 would shoot out like a giant rope. Then, when it hit the ground, the C4 would blow up and someone would have to tip toe through the little holes the grenades left and set up another backpack and continue doing this until we breached the minefields. So, obviously, our plans had changed between the day before and this day.

As night approached, we saddled up and got ready to move out. The Lieutenant said,

"Serocki you're point man."

"Aye, aye sir", I said.

It got dark and we headed out. After we had humped a distance we started hearing gunfire ahead of us, not too far away. My heart began pounding again and my breathing increased, I started moving rather expediently towards the gunfire.

The Lieutenant started yelling at me to slow down, but I kept going. He then ordered me to stop, so I did. He came up to me and said,

"We can't go that fast, those three carrying those one hundred pound backpacks can't keep up. Those fucking things are heavy."

"Aye, aye sir, but there's a fire fight going on up there and we have to get up there and help our boys."

"Don't worry Serocki we will get there."

So we started off again, but I do not think I went any slower, I had to get up there. It was like something clicked in my brain. I just started reacting. I was reacting just as I was trained to do. We trained so much in peace time that everything was just a natural reaction now. We have a saying for that in the Corps. It goes like this, "The more you sweat in peace, the less you bleed in war". God, I sure had hoped that was true!

Eve of Destruction

We finally made it up to the firefight in a matter of minutes. It was completely dark out now. We were told to spread out and get in holes and wait for orders. We were right there on the front lines with the grunts. Bullets and tracer rounds (bullets that glow so you can see them at night) were flying over my hole like crazy. It resembled a firefight with lasers from the movie "Star Wars". I then heard mortar fire coming from the Iraqi's location. I could feel the shells impact the sand. The earth shook and the sand fell on me, I would flinch and my hands would start to shake. I just remember hearing things whiz by overhead, mortar shells slamming the ground, and trying to bury myself as deep as I could in my hole, like a gopher. Mother nature and I were getting quite friendly.

The grunts opened up fire with six M60 machine guns. They perform this tactic called dragon teeth. All the guns move from left to right, or vise versa, and move up and down in unison and just spray a wall of lead with six guns that shoot about two hundred rounds a minute. That pretty much silenced the Iraqis. "These must have been the assholes who called the fucking artillery in on us", I thought. "Well, they're getting theirs now!"

They started coming across the minefields in rows. So, we started marking the places were they were walking. That way, we were aware of the locations that were safe to cross the minefield. While we were doing this one of our trucks started rolling through one of the wider paths we had made and BAM! It got to close to the edge and hit a land mine. We all hit the deck. Luckily no one was hurt, except the truck.

When we got to the other side of the minefield we rounded up approximately fifteen hundred prisoners. There were only a couple hundred of us. We were now in between two minefields, which joined at one end to form a "V" shape.

Next we started setting up one of those C4 backpacks on the edge of the next minefield. We had to blow paths through for Task Force Ripper (1st Marine Division, 7th Marines) who was to come by at six in the morning, which was only a few hours from now. It was problematic trying to set something up we never saw before, let alone had any training with, in complete darkness! Especially since we did not know what was waiting for us on the other side of this minefield!

We finally got the first backpack set up and detonated it. The C4 rope shot out and laid straight out in the minefield like it was supposed to, but it did not blow up! "It fucking figures, damn it! Typical government. Always giving us fucked up, half ass shit to try out in combat when our lives are at stake and the shit don't even work!"

So, we set up the next one. It fired out into the minefield like the last one. However, this time, three of the C4 grenades blew up.

"Well, at least they're getting better."

"Yeah the next one ought to have at least six grenades blow up!"

Someone tip-toed out through the three tiny holes the grenades made and carefully set up the next one and fired it off. This time only one grenade blew up. "Fuck this shit, man!"

The Staff Sergeant called us back and while we were doing that the grunts used a tank with a plow blade on the front of it (like a bull dozer) and cleared a wide enough path for the vehicles to get through. The Staff Sergeant said that we would remain here for the rest of the night and wait for Task Force Ripper to come through in two more hours. "Damn", I thought, "It was already four in the morning. I hadn't eating anything since early afternoon or slept since the day before." I wasn't hungry or tired though. I was too pumped with adrenaline.

The grunts moved further down to our left off into the horizon. It was just the engineers now, about twenty or so, with M-16 rifles and a radio. We started digging in and putting on our chemical warfare suits (a once piece suit with gloves and rubber boots) and prepared for the worst.

By the time we were done with our plan and putting on our chemical suits, the sun was just starting to rise. I broke out my entrenching tool and started digging a fighting hole. It seemed as though I was one of very few who decided to actually carry their e-tool. Most of us, when we got sent on this mission, discarded everything except food, water and most importantly ammo.

While I was digging and watching the sunrise over my new home, Rollins, a boot (new guy) from Virginia, came over and asked if he could use my e-tool when I was done. I said, "yeah, sure." So, he sat and we talked while I dug. After I had been digging a little while, we heard this noise in the sky. It kind of sounded like a jet engine, but only much smaller. We both looked up, but there were no planes in the sky.

All of a sudden, we heard this thump in a berm of dirt about ten yards behind us. We both looked and saw a large tank or artillery round impaled in the birm. Nothing happened; it did not explode. Rollins and I both looked at each other and said, "What the fuck was that!" We looked out to the horizon and saw nothing.

So, I went back to digging and he went back to talking to me. A few minutes later we heard the same noise and the same thump again. We both looked in the berm and saw another round, which did not explode either. "Damn, that's two fucking rounds that landed next to us and didn't explode!" I thought to myself, "My luck has got to run out soon." We both started laughing at what had just happened and we looked off into the horizon again. This time, however, we saw tanks! I then gave Rollins my e-tool and he ran and started digging faster than he ever dug before. He looked like a dog that was frantically digging a hole under a fence, trying to escape out of the yard.

The next thing you know the tanks started shooting their machine guns, which were equivalent to a fifty-caliber machine gun. There were rounds flying all over the place. Before my brain even registered what was happening a tracer round flew right in front of my face, so close I felt the heat on my nose. I actually heard the bullet spinning as it flew in front of my face. I yelled, "holy fuck!" Once again, I became one with Mother Nature. Once I did that, all hell broke loose. They were shooting all kinds of things at us. They had us all pinned down. I heard tank rounds exploding, bullets zinging overhead by the thousands. There were ricochets, thumps and explosions. The ground was shaking again. I started shaking. It was like I was in an earthquake. My head hurt as though I had fallen down and slammed it on the concrete. I have never been so scared in my life.

Randal came running over and leaped into my hole. In mid air he said, "Serocki, can I get in your hole with you?" He then landed on top of me. I was lying on my back. Things were blowing up all around us and bullets were whizzing by over the hole. Hunt, who was from Oklahoma, came running over and got behind the berm I had made with the dirt I dug out of my hole. Randal grabbed a hold of my leg and I grabbed his and we both started screaming, "Jesus Christ don't let us fucking die!" Every time something hit, dirt fell in the hole and the ground shook.

Everything was so loud and so confusing. It was like being under water during the night with no lights, being out of oxygen and not knowing which way was up to the surface. Hunt kept lifting his head up over the berm trying to talk to us. "Hunt keep your fucking head down or your gonna loose the mother-fucker!" It was so confusing. I could not think. I did not know where I was, what was going on, or what to do. I thought everyone was dying.

Earl, from Idaho, was with the Staff Sergeant and Corporal Brooks. He was on the radio screaming, "We're getting pounded, and we're pinned down and can't move. We need an air strike or something, over." All I could hear was static on the radio. No one would answer us. We were all alone, hung out to dry.

Earl started screaming louder on the radio, "Jesus Christ you mother-fuckers we need an air strike; help us out Goddamn it! We're fucking pinned down and we're all gonna die." Still, there was nothing. All that came back was static. "You stupid cocksuckers", Earl yelled. Then, as fast as it started, it all stopped. It was dead silent. Corporal Brooks started yelling out our names one by one and asking if everyone was all right. Amazingly, no one was injured.

Then Corporal Brooks said, "Lets get the fuck outta here. C'mon lets go, damn it!" I got out of that hole and started running in my chemical warfare suit through the sand. It felt like I was running in slow motion.

I did not even know what I was doing, where I was going or anything. I was just running. All I could hear was my heart beating and my breathing. Then, faintly, I heard Corporal Brooks yelling,

"Serocki, what the fuck are you doing?" He yelled it over and over again.

"Serocki, what the fuck are you doing?"

"Serocki, what the fuck are you doing?"

I could barely hear it, but I kept on running and then all of a sudden I just stopped. I turned around and said,

"I am getting the fuck out of here like you said."

"You're about to step in the mine field."

I looked down at my feet and right in front of my foot was a land mine. "Jesus Christ, I've almost died like four fucking times today", I thought. My heart sank to my stomach and I felt all the blood rush to my gut. Then it was as if I had snapped out of it and I came back to the world.

The shooting started again. I looked for a place to hide, I was out in the open now and I surely would be cut to pieces. To my left was a huge berm the tank plow had made the night before. I ran for it and got down on the ground between the two berms and once again, I became one with Mother Nature. I thought to myself, "How the fuck did I not see this a few minutes ago." I was just so confused I did not know what the hell was going on or what I was doing. I could not think. There was not enough time to think. I had to just react.

The bullets were flying overhead again. As I was looking off into the horizon I saw one of our trucks speeding through the desert. The tanks were zeroing in on it. The driver stopped the truck and got out. He started running and one of the machine gun bullets from the tanks caught him somewhere around the waste and split him in half like a head on a guillotine. "Holy fuck" I thought and I buried my head in my arms.

The shooting stopped and we got up and started running again, towards where the grunts were. A dump truck, one of ours, was driving by and we hitched a ride. We all piled into the back and drove on passing Iraqi bunker complexes. I held my rifle tight, locked and loaded, keeping aim on those bunkers. We stopped in an Iraqi bunker complex that had been abandoned. There were numerous fighting holes there. Staff Sergeant told us to take up residence in the holes for now and await our next orders.

Hunt, Randal and I were in one fighting hole together. We were lying on our backs and the roof over this thing almost touched our noses. There were slits to see out of. We were all looking at each other and not saying a thing. I wanted to just break down and cry, but I could not. I had to suck it up and press on. The rest of the world was counting on us. I knew my mom wanted me to come home and so did I. My hands were still shaking. The Staff Sergeant came by asking all of us how we were. I said, "ooh-rah Staff Sergeant." Of course I was faking my enthusiasm. I was just trying to hold it together. I would not admit to myself I was scared. I could not be. The other two did not say anything.

The media had put its tentacles out and retrieved their story about the events that consumed our lives those few arduous days. Here is their story as they portrayed it:

The Arizona Republic
GIs were in Kuwait days before land war
By Michael R. Gordon
The New York Times

JUBAIL, Saudi Arabia – Two days before the official beginning of the allied ground attack on Iraqi forces, more than 3,000 U.S. Marines secretly moved more than 10 miles into Kuwait to prepare for the land war, senior Marine Officers say.

The Marine Corps operation constituted the beginning of the preliminary phase of the land campaign, even before president Bush issued an ultimatum to Iraqi President Saddam Hussein to get out of Kuwait.

While withholding many details, American military officials have acknowledged that U.S. forces had conducted raids across the border before the official start of the ground war. But the Marine operation, disclosed by officials at a desert camp for the 1st Division north of Jubail, was much larger than the cross-border operations described earlier.

The Marine action was not a quick raid that took U.S. forces across the border and back, but the opening wedge of a drive toward Kuwait City, Kuwait.

"My instructions were to do nothing that is irreversible but to be able to execute," Maj. Gen. Mike Myatt, the commander of the 1st Marine Division, said in a briefing at the camp in northern Saudi Arabia.

Myatt was referring to orders from Army Gen. J. Norman Schwarzkopf, commander of allied forces in the Persian Gulf War.

"I was a little concerned because I already had Task Force Grizzly and Task Force Taro into Kuwait," Myatt said, referring to Marine forces that were about 12 miles into Kuwait. "But I thought that is all reversible. We can just bring them out."

The task of the 1st and 2nd Marine Divisions, and other allied units, was to keep Iraqi troops preoccupied in southern Kuwait until the allies surprised the Iraqis with the main attack through Iraq. But the Marine forces moved more swiftly into Kuwait than expected, defeating early Iraqi counterattacks. Though accorded a secondary role, the Marine thrust took them in four days, to the gates of Kuwait City.

The 1st Marine Division planned to use speed and deception to "unhinge" the Iraqi forces and avoid a costly war of attrition in Kuwait.

"The mission was to defeat the Iraqis, not to destroy them," Myatt said in the briefing to his troops.

"There is quite a difference. If we were there to destroy them, we would probably still be there trying to root out every Iraqi position. But we can defeat him by getting in behind him, causing him to collapse, and moving quickly to unhinge him. Speed was very important."

The Marines were to break through the teeth of Iraq's front-line defenses.

The Iraqis had constructed two main sets of defensive barriers.

The first set was about 12 miles inside Kuwait. Most of the Iraqi front-line troops were behind the second set of barriers, eight miles further back. The Iraqi plan was to use the barriers to slow the allied advance while their artillery pounded at them.

To destroy the Iraqi artillery, the Marines fired their own artillery at the Iraqi positions while a Marine spotter plane directed airstrikes at newly revealed Iraqi artillery positions. Fuel-air explosives, which spray a mist of fuel into the air that is then ignited, were dropped on Iraqi front-line positions, said Marine Col. Jim Fulks, commander of Task Force Grizzly.

Marine commanders expected that these attacks would do serious damage to the Iraqi front-line positions, but to ensure that their main attack could slice through these defenses, they decided to send two infantry task forces into Kuwait before the official start of the ground war.

The units would sneak up to the Iraq fortification in order to direct American artillery and airstrikes, then slip through minefields and barbed wire to attack the Iraqi front-line troops from behind. They also would use explosives to blast a path through the minefields so that Task Force Ripper, the lead Marine mechanized unit, could pass swiftly through the Iraqi front lines.

As the start of the ground war approached, the infantry task forces began to deploy under darkness, slipping into Kuwait at one point during a rainstorm.

"We moved into Kuwait and literally took and secured 20 kilometers (about 13 miles) two days before the ground offensive," Fulks said.

The task force's effort to find a path through the mines was complicated by continuing allied airstrikes against the Iraqis in front of them. The Marines said they could not get a message through to stop the bombardment so their engineers could work.

But then came a lucky break.

A company of Iraqi soldiers left their dug-in positions behind the mines and gave up, braving mortar fire from other Iraqis trying to prevent them from surrendering.

The Iraqis helped the task force mark a path through the minefields and disclosed that a belt of anti-personnel mines had been laid behind the anti-tank explosives. The Marines had not known about these anti-personnel mines. But the Iraqis did not know a route through the field.

Sgt. Charles Restifo, a combat engineer from Phoenix, began to forge a path through the anti-personnel mines by prodding with a bayonet.

"What is really scary and eerie is moving through a minefield at night knowing that if you take a step in the wrong direction, you could be ending your life," Fulks said.

Eve of Destruction

The sky was all gray and it started raining. The chemical suits we were wearing were British. They were the best of the line. However, if it rained they were rendered ineffective. "It fucking figures", I thought. The rain and wind would, however, help us out if we did get gassed by blowing it back into the Iraqi's faces, something I would not have minded watching.

You could see all of the oil field fires burning, pouring jet-black smoke into the dismal gray sky. The smoke gave everything a greenish-gray hue. It rose to the sky and stayed there forming a blanket over our battlefield. The smell of gunpowder, burning petroleum, and death hovered in the air penetrating their way into my nose and lungs. It was hard to breath. The air was so thick with smoke that it made me cough constantly.

There were blown up bunkers, burnt out shells of tanks, dead bloated Iraqis and many of their miscellaneous body parts littering the desert. "Everything was just black." I thought, "just like it say's in that Rolling Stones song "Painted Black". It looked like a landscape of burnt marshmallows. It was now somewhere near eleven a.m. I figured. I still had not eaten or slept, nor did I feel like either. My stomach was nauseous and I was high on adrenaline. For the time being we just sat and waited for our next orders.

We loaded back up in the dump truck after a while and then headed north. We stopped at a location and got out of the truck. Some other Marines were here rounding up the fifteen hundred prisoners we took earlier in the day and they were moving them out. I picked up my M16 and gripped it tightly and glared at the pitiful looking Iraqis. I was so pissed at them for causing all of this. I wanted to kill them all. The Lieutenant must have been able to tell what I was thinking because he said, "At ease Serocki." I just said, "Aye, aye sir."

We were then told to start digging in. There were forty more Iraqi tanks rolling our way. "Great, how the fuck are the twenty or so of us, armed with M16's, going to stop fucking Russian tanks?"

Actually, we had devised some methods for just such a case. We were taught to improvise, overcome and adapt. Never give up! Mission completion always comes first! No matter what the cost. We had made Molotov cocktails out of bottles, fuel and Styrofoam. The idea was to throw these at the tanks and they would catch on fire. The Styrofoam would melt and act like glue and make the flames stick to the tank. This in turn, would cause the tank to get hot and in theory the enemy soldiers would come flying out of there. Then, we would pick them off one by one, like we were dove hunting.

We also were digging holes to hide in and then placing anti-tank mines on pieces of cardboard. We would attach string to the cardboard and run it back to our holes and hide in them. Then if the tanks came by we would pull the string that was attached to the cardboard, and hence, the mines, in front of the tanks. These mines had tall skinny rods sticking out the top of them. If a tank rolled over it and bent the rod forty-five degrees, the mine would shoot up through the belly of the tank and once inside, it would explode.

Finally, some people were assigned the job of taking these same mines without the rods, prime them to explode, and run up to the back of the tank and place the mine upside down on top of the engine compartment and run like hell. Again, when it exploded those who lived through it would come out of the tank and one by one we would pick them off. It was kill or be killed.

The Iraqis were very afraid of the Marines and justly so! They thought just to be eligible to go to Marine Corps boot camp, a person had to kill one of his own family members.

So, we used this to our advantage of course. At one point an Iraqi prisoner had asked me what family member I had killed. I said, "My sister, while my mother was still pregnant with her." I swear the poor guy about died on the spot.

Most of them could speak very good English. As a matter of fact, one of the Iraqi soldiers was not really an Iraqi. He was a Saudi who had come home to visit his parents in Kuwait and Saddam took him and put him in his army, as he did to so many other Saudi's and Kuwaiti's. He had old men and young sixteen-year-old kids in his army fighting against us.

People are always so quick to judge and say things like, "How can you kill boys and old men?" What they fail to realize is if you do not shoot them I guarantee, he will kill you. I was not about to die here. I made my mind up that I would kill anything that lived, walked, crawled, or breathed that was not a U.S. soldier. This attitude is what changed me. It was constantly drilled into our heads. I had finally succumbed to it because I had realized that I must adopt this ideology in order to survive. This way of thinking is not an inherent human characteristic. I had to change from a human into an inhuman. I wanted to come home. I knew this change would have drastic effects on me once I did come home. However, I would deal with that then. For now, my mission was to come home and to kill anything in my path that would try to stop me from achieving that goal. Death is hard to come to terms with. It is hard to accept. But, you have to do it or you will die. You have to get rid of that fear of dying, that moral sense not to kill. You must overcome these mental roadblocks so they will not cloud your mind at that moment when it is either him or me.

We waited for a while but the tanks never came. We were still on the outskirts of a major bunker complex. Our next orders were to clear it out and blow up anything that was left. We all split up into teams of a couple guys each. The grunts were going from bunker to bunker clearing them out.

I was following four grunts up to a bunker. We were all crouched down as we approached. The lead Marine was yelling in Arabic for anyone to come out of the hole. We received no answer and no one came out. We approached the door of the bunker. As we did I noticed a trip wire going from one side of the entrance to the other. I yelled, "Stop! Booby trap!" Everyone stopped. I told them to clear out and I would clear the obstacle.

I low crawled up to it with the grunts covering me with their weapons pointed at the entrance. It was a very crude booby trap and all it required was for me to cut the wire to the explosive. I remember, as I was about to cut it, my hands were sweaty and my heart was beating again. I kept thinking, "What if I fuck up and blow everyone up? I guess it wouldn't matter much because we'd all be dead and outta here anyways." So, I closed my eyes, gritted my teeth, and cut the wire. I flinched and nothing happened.

The grunts were ecstatic that I cleared the obstacle and no one had blown up. Then, one of the grunts came up with a grenade and yelled, "Fire in the hole" and chucked it in the bunker. We all ran and it blew up and pieces flew everywhere. This was happening all over the bunker complex. Marines were approaching bunkers and instead of wasting time, they were chucking grenades into the bunkers and waiting for the explosions.

One grunt threw a grenade into a bunker, it blew up and blew the front part of his foot off. The bunkers, quite often, were full of explosives and bullets. It sounded, and looked, like the Fourth of July on steroids.

We came to the other side of the bunker complex and the engineers were gathering together with our Lieutenant.

The bunkers were still blowing up. Just then a bullet whizzed by my ear. I heard the bullet spinning again. I fell to the ground and pointed my rifle in the direction the bullet came from. I saw nothing except our own grunts walking the landscape, like ministers of death with tendrils of smoke rising behind them, bright flashes illuminating their dirty worn, torn silhouettes, they were screaming and yelling as they continued to clear trenches and bunkers. "It must have been a stray bullet."

There was one more bunker over by us so the Lieutenant and I went to clear it out. We made it inside and no one was in there. We found a whole pile of AK47's in there. In this same location was a huge gatling gun that shot fifty-caliber shells and a one hundred twenty millimeter mortar, which is like a cannon. It took two of us to lift up one shell. The Lieutenant picked up an AK47 and we had someone take a picture of us. Looking at the picture now I see a black face from the smoke, dirty fingernails, a hollow look on my face, and I think, "Is that really me?"

The next thing we had to do was blow up all of this equipment, ammo and explosives. So we went around and set up C-4 charges and backed off quite a ways. We then detonated everything and made one hell of an explosion. Our mission at this location was complete. Everything was destroyed in a matter of seconds by a handful of engineers and several grunts.

We loaded up the truck again and moved on. As evening was approaching we came upon an airport. As we were pulling up you could see that the place was half demolished. Buildings were on fire. Black smoke was billowing out of them. The air was thick. It was hard to breathe. The sky was dark, as if a big black luminous cloud hung over us. The ground and sky looked an orange-green color. It looked a lot like the sky does just before a tornado hits. All of a sudden horns started honking and I turned around and looked behind the dump truck we were riding in and the HMMV behind us was flashing its lights and honking its horn.

The Marines inside were giving the universal symbol for gas, which is touching your shoulders with your fists and raising your arms again only from the elbows up. "Holy shit, we're getting gassed. Gas, gas, gas!" We all became frantic. We heard explosions. They were delivering the gas through artillery shells we figured. I grabbed my mask out of its pouch and put it on my head. I placed my hands over the sides of it and blew out to get rid of any gas that may have gotten trapped inside the mask. Then, I placed my hands on the front of the mask, about where your mouth is, and sucked to create a seal.

While I was doing this, Banks, who was from Texas, was panicking. He kept grabbing my arm and yelling, "Help me Serocki, help me. I can't get my mask on." I wanted to help him right away, but my brain very quickly recalled my training. Which taught me to always take care of myself first and then help the others. So, that is what I did.

Banks was still panicking and yelling at me. Then I got angry and I grabbed him by his shirt with both of my hands and slammed him into the back of the dump truck cab and said, "Calm the fuck down Banks or you will die. I'll help you. Get you fucking mask on." So he did and I helped him get his gloves on. He thanked my repetitively. I said, "No problem brother." Just then it got pitch black. I could not see a thing. I put my hand in front of my face and I literally could not see it. I thought, "Awe fuck man, I inhaled some gas and I blacked out. Now I'm dying". My heart was pounding again. I was so scared. I was waiting to go into convulsions like they said we would and I started looking for my

Atropene injector. These are tubes that look like pens that have a needle and Atropene in them. When you slam it against something, like your leg, the needle pops out and into you and injects the Atropene. All this does is slow down the nerve reaction to buy you some more time to get you to a hospital. We also had Valium injectors to slow down your nerve responses, which would slow down the effects of the nerve gas.

While I was going through all of this I heard others in the back of the dump truck saying, "Awe fuck, I inhaled the gas." Then I said, " I can't see either. We're ok, it's just dark as hell. Quick, someone find a chemlite, crack it, stick it in the bottom of the truck so we have something to look at and we won't panic." So Johnson did just that. It made us all feel better. We had something to look at.

There was so much destruction and so many fires burning here that it was starting to get dark very early in the day. So dark, that you really could not even see the hand in front of your face. As time went on, it would get light at around six or seven a.m. and be completely dark by ten a.m.

Then it all ended. The threat of gas was over and the grunts had cleared the airport. We all were allowed to take off our masks. We were told we would stay here for a while so we should eat something and try to get some sleep. This would be our only chance for a while most likely. Here I was, two days without eating or sleeping and I had been through hell. I felt like I had just walked through Satan's front door and I was dancing with him. Teetering on the edge of death and the brink of insanity. The landscape was black, filled with smoke. Everything was destroyed. We were the only things left alive on the landscape. It looked like World War III had just occurred. It was as if I was in a world of black and gray shadows, interrupted by flashes of fire and brimstone, and I heard noises as the Bible says, "weeping and gnashing of teeth" and surrounded by death.

We were told to stay close to the truck because there were land mines around. So I picked out a spot by the rear tire. I really was not even hungry, nor did I feel like sleeping. I was running on pure adrenaline. I did not know when I would have a chance to eat or sleep again so I thought I had better choke something down and at least lay down. I ate a quick MRE and laid down, using my gas mask as a pillow.

The next thing you know the rare moment of quietness that I was experiencing, although I would not say peaceful, was pierced by loud shouts of, "gas, gas, gas." "Damn those motherfuckers", I thought. It was so dark you could not see anything. I had no idea what time it was either. It was like being in one never ending day. Janice Joplin summed it up when she said, in one of her songs, "It's all the same fucking day man."

I quickly grabbed my gas mask and quit breathing, so I would not suck in any gas. I put it on and put my hands on the bottom part of the mask to begin to dawn and clear (the action of clearing any gas out of your mask that was trapped in it when you put it on) and I felt glass. "Holy fuck", I thought, "I put my damn mask on upside down!" I quickly took it off and put it on the right way. My heart was racing and I was freaking out. I hoped I did not inhale any gas, but I suppose that I would find out soon enough. My hands were sweaty as I clutched my weapon and my Atropene injector kit, hoping I would never have to use it. Then as quickly as it started it was over again.

By this time we had received new orders and were moving on. We left this location and by daylight we ended up at another airport. It was dark and cloudy again and the wind was blowing with a slight drizzle in the air. The clouds took on an orange-green appearance again. It certainly looked like a day of reckoning. All the oilfield fires were burning still. All the things we had blown up along the way were still burning. The whole area from horizon to horizon was filled with black smoke stacks, which looked like black tornadoes closing in on us. The landscape was filled with destroyed tanks, bunker complexes, equipment, and burnt, mangled bodies. Pieces of bodies and whole bloated bodies were all around us. The combination of these smells permeated the air. I will never forget the smell of death. Since my time here, I have never smelled anything like it. It is so overwhelmingly horrid that it instantly makes you want to vomit.

We got out of our dump truck that we had commandeered since the beginning of our little tour of the Kuwait border. We occupied some foxholes the grunts had dug, but were no longer occupied. The grunts were attacking the airport and we were just on the outside of it waiting for them to call us in to get them out of a jam. Then the call came. They wanted us to blow a hole through the three rows of chain link fence that surrounded the airport so they could get more men through in a hurry. I remembered in school they told us our life expectancy in combat was about eight to eleven seconds. I was about to find out if that would become a reality or not.

Corporal Brooks, another Marine and myself were to blow up the fence. Corporal Brooks had been preaching the whole time not to use too much demo. He then said to use a whole satchel charge of C4. Bullets were flying overhead and the Iraqi's were shooting rocket propelled grenades at us (RPG's). They are grenades that go on the end of their AK47's and when you pull the trigger the bullet hits a primer at the back of the grenade and it shoots off like a rocket.

A Line In the Sand

We kept telling him we do not need that much C4 and he just yelled back, "Just prime the fucking satchel charge and lets go!" So we did. We stuck a blasting cap in one of the sticks of C4 and left a fuse on it, about six seconds worth, and an M-1 fuse igniter.

We got up out of the hole we were in. All three of us ran toward the rows of chain link fences. The bullets were still whizzing by and the RPG's were exploding around us. We made it to the fence and pulled the fuse igniter and set the bag up against the fence and ran like hell. All of a sudden all twenty-one and one-quarter pound sticks of C4 blew up. We were still running away and then I heard someone screaming. It was Corporal Brooks. We ran back to get him. We asked him where he was hit. He said, "In my calf." He had blood on one of his calves so we helped him back to our hole. When we got back we arranged for him to be seen by a corpsman and he was taken off to a field hospital.

Now we were without a squad leader. "Holy shit, I made it without being hit by anything", I thought. I looked over at the fence and we blew it six ways from Sunday and the grunts were going through it. The bullets and RPG rounds were still whizzing by. They got inside and starting clearing buildings, building by building. The shelling of our positions stopped. At one point we saw the grunts in a firefight. As we were watching we noticed both sides were shooting red tracer-rounds. The Iraqi's had green. We got on the radio immediately and notified them that Marines were shooting at other Marines. Luckily, we found out later, no one had gotten hurt.

Next, they attached four engineers to each squad of infantry. From that point one engineer was assigned to one grunt fire-team, which consists of four Marines. I was attached to four grunts that drove a tow missile HMMV. There was not enough room for me to sit in the HMMV, it only sat four and had a turret in the middle of it. So, I sat on the hood on the passenger side. "Great", I thought, "here I go again, attached to four guys I don't know and I am going to be fighting side by side with them. I don't know how they will react. I guess I will just have to rely on my training and do what I know how to do."

Finally, we rolled out into the grayish-green daylight of a cloudy, smoke filled desert battlefield, once again. It was non-stop. We were constantly on the move. Hit them hard and fast so we would confuse them.

We were approaching another bunker complex in the distance when we stopped. We all got out of the vehicle and I got off of the hood. The Sergeant came over and gave us our orders. Our orders put us on the right side of the bunker complex. We were to go into it and clear it out. The five of us approached the bunker complex. There were bunkers everywhere, connected in some spots with trenches. Some trenches were straight and others were shaped like long rows of W's. The bunkers were mostly underground. Approximately two or three feet of the tops of the bunkers were showing above the ground. These bunkers were huge. They were like little fortresses that withstood all of our bombing.

The closer we got, we began to see bloated dead bodies scattered across the battlefield. The stench was disgusting! We did not see any Iraqis once we got close, so the Sergeant told us each to take a bunker. I thought, "Awe fuck, I don't want to go in there!" But, I had too. I approached the bunker and I got my pistol out (the one which the Captain gave me) and my flashlight. I turned the flashlight on and held it against the barrel of the gun. I entered the doorway of the bunker and wiggled down the dark tunnel. My heart was racing, pounding so hard I thought it was going to pop out of my chest! The veins in my neck were throbbing, and bulging, the blood was pumping so fast. I felt nervous, just like I used to when I played hide and seek as a kid. I guess it was the anticipation of what I would find in the bunker.

I got to the bottom of the bunker and popped up on one knee and quickly scanned the room. As I was scanning to the right I came across an Iraqi soldier sitting in the sand. I thought "Holy fucking shit!" He froze and I pumped fifteen rounds from my pistol into him. I just kept pulling the trigger. Click, click, click. I was out of ammo, but I kept pulling the trigger, I could not stop. My hands starting shaking and then my body followed. I was holding my breath and then all of a sudden I let it out and started panting.

"Are you alright down there, hey, are you fucking ok?" The Sergeant was yelling down to see if I was ok. He must have heard the shots. I snapped out of it. And said, "Yeah, I'm fine."

"All right, then check out the rest of the bunker and get the fuck outta there. We gotta keep moving."

"Aye, aye Serge."

I went over to the Iraqi just to make sure he was dead. I did not want anymore surprises. I did not think my heart could take it. He was dead all right. "What have I done?" I thought. He had several holes in his shirt and he sure as hell was not breathing. I took his beret and stuffed it in my pocket.

On one side of the bunker there was a queen size bed, a dresser, and a footlocker. The bed had purple satin sheets on it. There were items scattered all over the place. "Son of a cock sucking bitch, the mother-fucker was living better off than me!" I could not believe it. He had a bed with purple satin sheets! I went over to his footlocker. It was up against a wall. I went behind the wall and reached around the edge of it and flipped open his footlocker. I hid behind the wall just incase the footlocker was booby-trapped. I clenched my teeth and closed my eyes as it opened, but nothing happened. "Damn, that was fucking stupid", I thought.

So, I got up and went over to inspect what was inside the footlocker. Inside I found a small book with a squad in it and all of their pictures. Some of the pictures were torn out. "Those ones must have got fucking wasted", I thought. Then, I found two other books with pictures of bombs and land mines with descriptions. All three books had writing in them, but it was all in Arabic. I could not read any of it. All I knew how to say in Arabic was, "Come out with your hands up Mother-Fucker and put your weapon down cocksucker." As far as I was concerned that was enough. That is all I needed to know.

I grabbed the books and I found his backpack. I put the books in his backpack and grabbed his AK47 magazine pouch. He also had a black Republican Guard beret, so I took that too. I found a picture of him with his wife or girlfriend and I kept that to. I stuffed everything in his backpack. I thought to myself, "I must have killed a fucking general or something, cool!" I then got out of there. I climbed back up the tunnel and met up with the Sergeant and the other four Marines. We piled back into the HMMV and I got on the hood.

We drove to the next set of bunkers and trenches. I was holding my M16 and looking at all the sand on it. "Next chance I get I have to get this thing clean." Then next thing you know I see three or four rows of Iraqi soldiers in a formation marching toward us. "What the fuck are those assholes doing", I thought. "Well, I'm not gonna wait around to find out." I pointed my rifle at them and pulled the trigger. Nothing happened. "Damn it! The mother-fucker is jammed!" I looked at the ejection port and the bullet was jammed, due to all the sand no doubt. I started frantically smacking a button on the back right side of the rifle, which sends the bolt home and the bullet where it needs to be.

I pointed the rifle again and pulled the trigger. This time it fired. So, I pulled the trigger again. "Mother-fucker! It goddamn jammed again." I did the same thing again. "I guess this is how I will have to fight this one. One shot one kill. Adapt, overcome and improvise Marine! The HMMV slowed down and I jumped off the hood and crouched down in the sand next to it. The other grunts got out and we started assaulting the bunker complex.

The Iraqi's had not shot back yet. I thought, " I don't see any recognizable signs of surrender, so I'm gonna keep on shooting ragheads." Just then a HMMV pulls up behind us with an entourage. There is a major standing in the HMMV.

"Cease fire, cease fire! The war is over!"

"What the fuck do you mean the war is over", I thought.

Some one yelled, "Get the fuck down or you're gonna lose your head. We're about to get into it good!"

"I repeat, cease fire!"

"Could that be why the Iraqis weren't shooting? They knew something we didn't. What the fuck took them so long to tell us?"

Amidst all the confusion, we gathered up our units and we got in our vehicles and went back to a rally point in the rear and I joined back with my original unit. I still could not believe it. "Is the war really over? How long have I been out here fighting?" I did not even know. I had no concept of time. It did not matter to me. I thought in sequences of when is our next fire-fight? It is hard to keep track of time when it gets pitch black at ten a.m. It seemed like someone was playing a chess game, we were the pawns and just as we were about to be moved into position to capture the queen, the person who was moving us around on the board was called to dinner. It ended just like that. I felt cheated. I had spent nearly a year of my life over here in order to rid the world of Saddam Hussein and his atrocities against humanity. Now, I had been robbed of completing my mission. It made me feel like it was all for nothing, like my government had used me for some political dog and pony show. The politicians acquired what they wanted and I lost my soul. I felt like I was left with unfinished business that I would never be able to finish.

12

BORN IN THE U.S.A.

Born down in a dead man's town. The first kick I took was when I hit the ground. You end up like a dog that's been beat too much, till you spend half your life just covering up.

By Bruce Springsteen and the E Street Band

Our campsite was still inside Kuwait. We were not too far back from where we just were. We set up a big piece of canvas we found with a few tall cammie-net poles to hold it up. The Lieutenant had a briefing and told us that we may be here for about thirty days just to make sure nothing happens and Saddam keeps his tail between his legs. "Great", I thought, "Now I am going to have to sit here in this fucking sand nigger land for another fucking month. They will probably forget about us and leave us here for another six months. How could they play with us like that? The war is over. I have been here almost a year and fought the war. Let us go home and replace us with some fresh bodies from the real world."

Well, it was back to finding ways to pass the time again so we all would not go crazy. I think it was easier before when we had no idea when we were going home, when we would fight, or how long it was going to last. Now that the war was over, and we could see light at the end of the tunnel, it was much harder to wait. I thought it was like having to go to the bathroom really bad and you know it is going to be forty miles to the next rest stop, and you endure. However, when you get to that sign that says, "rest stop next exit", you suddenly cannot wait.

One night we built a campfire ring and made a fire. We were in the middle of an area where there were blown up tanks and trucks, dead, bloated, burnt, mutilated bodies and body parts lying around. There were also a few bunkers and trenches. Pieces of all kinds of things had been scattered everywhere. We used whatever we could scrounge up to build a fire.

The next day we went searching around. We entered this bunker complex and checked things out just to be sure there was nobody alive and to see if we could find some cool souvenirs. For most of us, our boots had had it. They were falling off of our feet. I had the soles of mine duck taped to the leather. My Korean buddy Laom was worse than anyone else. We had no more duck tape. So, we made it our mission to find him some new boots.

As we were searching through the dead bodies we came across a bloated fellow. He was a kind of a greenish-blue hue and stiff as a board. His belly looked like it was ready to pop. We thought he would make a cool picture. So a couple of us held up the body and someone took the picture. We all laughed as we dropped him on the sand after we had our fun. We found several legs, arms and hands scattered about the area. With some we tried to figure out what piece belonged to whom. It was like doing a giant real-life jigsaw puzzle.

Finally, I found a dead Iraqi with an exceptional pair of boots.

"Laom, what fucking size boot do you wear?"

"An eight."

"Well, I'll be a son-of-a-bitch. Today's your lucky day man. This fucker has brand new boots on and they are a size eight."

Laom came over and we took the boots off of the dead guy's feet. After all, he was not going to need them any more.

I thought to myself about everything I had seen recently. I could not believe it. The Iraqi's were living in bunkers fit for kings. They had real beds and everything. They had brand new boots and their uniforms were new, without holes, rips, tears or stained black from all the oil field fires. Here we were, stuck in the middle of the desert left to fend for ourselves until some one came and picked us up. Our boots were falling off of our feet, my uniform looked like Santa's cloak all stained with soot. The seat of my pants was completely ripped out and hanging there. My face was black, my fingers and nails were black. I had enough sand in my hair to build a sand box. My socks could stand up and walk on their own and to top it off I had not had a shower in several months, unless it rained. We were reduced to living like animals, finding a way to survive, any way we could. They were living like king Fajad himself.

After Laom fastened his boots upon his feet I thought, "God, I can't wait to get home and have a cold brew, eat a steak, crank up the radio and go down to the beach and find a hot broad to stay the weekend with. Even just to go to the beach and see real women half naked in bathing suits would be great at this point. Shit, I haven't even seen a picture of a woman in at least a month."

We walked over to a trench and jumped in. We walked it single file, rifles at the ready. We came to a bunker, rushed inside and the room was clear. Much to our surprise however, the room was filled with makeup, women's dresses, baby toys and so on. I could not believe it. The guy had his whole family with him. "What kind of sick fucker would bring his whole family to war with him? These are some retarded fucking bastards." I was glad we killed a bunch of them and cleansed the gene pool a bit.

We decided to take three of the dresses back to camp with us. That night we built a campfire. Three guys volunteered to put the dresses on. The Lieutenant was one of them. He chose the purple dress. Then, we each had to take turns asking the three in dresses to dance. We had a transistor radio with us and we turned it up as loud as it would go, which was not very loud. We figured we better get some practice asking chicks to dance so when we get back to the real world, we will not be lost. Hell, none of us had talked too a real woman in almost a year now. We had a blast that night. We all danced and told stories about what we were going to do when we got home. Everyone pretty much had the same goal, get drunk and screw as many women as we could. After all, we had some catching up to do.

The next day we got up and started searching around the area again. We all took a souvenir AK47. They all had loaded magazines so we found an open area and we leaned a flack jacket up against a piece of wood. We wanted to see how effective it was against Russian ammo. We all walked off a distance and lit the flack jacket up like a Christmas tree. Needless to say, it did not hold up very well. It resembled Swiss cheese so to speak.

The next thing we found was a mini dirt bike for a kid. We started it up and we all took turns driving it around all day until it ran out of gas. Then, we went from blown up truck to blown up truck and finally found some gas. We siphoned it out with a piece of hose we found. The dirt bike was fun, but we got in trouble for riding it and had to put it a way. The only joy we found and they took that away from us too. We had just won a war for Christ sake, let us have some fun. But, that was not allowed to happen.

All we did after that was sit around, sleep and talk about home to pass the time. Finally, they came to pick us up. It had only been about a week or so that we were in this location, not thirty days as they originally told us. We were going back to the rear to prepare to go home. "God, I hope we're on the first fucking freedom bird outta here!"

We were then told we would be heading through Kuwait City. The engineers piled back into our old dump truck and we headed down the road, or what was left of it. We had to let the Saudi's and Egyptians roll through first and we followed after. It was thought to be politically correct that way. There we went again, letting politicians run the war instead of warriors. It really did not matter we all just wanted to get the hell out of that place of death and destruction, suffering, HELL!

We headed down the road. There was a driver up front and the Lieutenant, who was still wearing that purple dress. The rest of us were in the back. While we were still a little ways from town and a bunch of us had to urinate.

We started banging on the back window of the dump truck and yelled at the Lieutenant to pull over or we would all pop. We pulled over and all twenty-five of us got on line and relieved ourselves. Once we finished, the Lieutenant, still in that purple dress, said, "Watch this guys." He walked out into the street as two beamers (Mercedes Benz cars) full of Arabs were pulling up. When they got close enough the Lieutenant lifted up his dress and pointed his toe into the street and showed off his hairy leg!

We all busted up laughing. The beamer screeched to a halt and the dark tinted windows rolled down and a few Arabs with checkered diapers on their heads leaned out and started cursing at us in Arabic and shaking their fists. All at once, in unison, twenty-five Marines locked and loaded their rifles. The Arabs suddenly became pale, of all things, the windows rolled up and they sped off! We had a good laugh out of that one. At that moment the Lieutenant said, "When we get back to the rear base camp I am going to report to the Colonel in this dress. I am not taking if off until then!" "Ooorah, sir", we all shouted.

We all piled back into the dump truck and got back in the convoy and headed out down the road. Shortly thereafter, we started to get close to Kuwait City. We could see the buildings on the horizon. Then, the scenery worsened. The road was filled with pot-holes and just blown to hell. There were burnt out shells of trucks and all kinds of other vehicles. There were dead, burnt bodies strewn about, frozen in their last position in life by fire. There were pieces of bodies lying around, a hand here, an arm there and so on. This became known as the "road of death".

Everywhere you looked death lurked, you could not

get away from it. It was like it had become just another part of life to me. It was like another day at the office. I thought to myself this is what WWII must have been like only a lot worse. We did not see the enemy as much as I would have thought. We would get shot at by things so far away we could not see them. We could not return fire. We just had to take it. People did not just get wounded there; they got blown to pieces. I looked around at all the destruction and death as we drove on by. We all cracked jokes and felt good that the war was over and it was not us laying in the sand in fifteen different pieces.

The sky was still a gray-green color, like before a tornado. Fires were burning in the background. At this point I cannot even remember being able to smell anything, hear anything or feel anything. It was like all my senses were dead, like they had just become numb to this whole horrible mess.

Once we got into the city, we saw hundreds of people in the streets cheering. Some of them had guns and would shoot them in the air. This did not sit well with me. I had a good hold on my M16 so I could use it if I needed to. At this point, I was not going to trust anything that wore a diaper on its head. The town was blown to pieces also. Buildings were destroyed and rubble lined the streets. Our stroll through Kuwait City was over as fast as it begun. We were on our way back to our base camp to await a trip out of this place. "God I hate it here. It seems like I will never go home. This is what life will be like to me for the rest of my life." I did have some good friends and power here though. I was responsible for taking away life if I deemed it necessary. I guess I just was used to this. I then began to mumble the words to a song that was written by I.J. Stewart and T. Brock of Strangeways.

Billy left when he heard the call that he knew would come some day. Someone's fight he believed to be right, for freedom of lands far away, the battle cry and the beat of the drum, won the hearts of so many like him. There's no justice when you live by the gun, you can't turn back, there's no turning back. After the hurt is gone, I know I'll never run to the beat of the drum, and I know we can't be strong until we learn to give, we learn to live again. All alone as the shadows fall, you've lost all your will to survive. How could so many have been so wrong. Was it the glory or was it the pride? You don't know why you've gone this far, all you know is the fear of the gun. There's only pain when the love is gone, and you know it's wrong, you know it's wrong. As he looks out across the hills he knew he would never be the same. No battle cry, no beat of the drum, no turning back, no turning back.

We finally got back to base camp. We got assigned to a large canvass tent, kind of like the ones on Mash, but big enough to house a whole platoon (about forty guys). The Lieutenant was still wearing his pretty purple dress with his rifle slung over his shoulder. There he went, off to see the Colonel. He came back to us a while later in his cammies.

"What happened sir? Did the Colonel kick your ass and rip your dress off?"

"No, I reported to him in it and he asked me what the fuck I was wearing. I replied, a dress sir!"

We all cracked up laughing. The Lieutenant was all right in my book. Then the moment became somber again.

The Lieutenant told us we may be here as long as thirty days and they may decide to keep us here to guard the rear

Born in the U.S.A.

until everyone gets out. "Awe, mother-fucking cocksucker, eat a bag of shit. You're full of all kinds of good fucking news sir! Man, its one fuck in the ass after another. We just fought and won the war, let some other cocksucker just in from the real world stay here and let us go the fuck home!"

I could not believe it, another thirty days! That night we got out of control. We found a box of chemlites, shook them up, cracked them open and got in a huge fight with them. We had glowing chemicals all over us. Then, we threw it all over the roof inside of the tent so it would look like stars. The First Sergeant came in and ripped us a new one. We were all in deep trouble the next day. That night, however, we had fun. We all looked like we were poisoned by a nuclear power plant.

Over the next few weeks and days they constantly messed with us. I had to burn diesel fuel and human feces. I dug holes for the tubes we urinated in and moved them when the ground was saturated. Then, they told us we had to start polishing our boots again. "Fuck me man. We are in the middle of the world's biggest kitty litter box and they're worried about our boots being shined. For crying out fucking loud, leave us the fuck alone already. Damn!" Next we were told that all of our gear had to be cleaned in order for us to get it back to the real world. So, instead of having to clean gear, we all started burying our stuff in the sand. That took care of that problem.

After they messed with us so much we decided to do something about it. We all still had our Valium injectors for the nerve gas attacks. So, we took the injectors and poked them into our cigarettes. Once they dried we would smoke them and get a hell of a buzz. We had to do something to make it a little better than it was. Besides, what could they do? Shave our heads and send us to the Gulf!

The Gunny started finding all of these Valium injectors laying around the wooden box that was built for us to go to the bathroom in and around the trash pit. The Gunny decided it was time to collect all of our Atropene and Valium injectors. He did not get a lot of them back. Once we caught word of what he was going to do we all got stoned out of our gourd.

Finally, the last thing they could do to us, was to take back all of the Iraqi arms and ammunition that we seized. Most of it was stuff that we took for souvenirs. Johnson had a flare gun with the flares. Other people had bullets and some hand grenades. Johnson said "fuck it" and threw the flares into the trash pit at night. Someone dropped a grenade down the piss tube without pulling the pin. Others threw bullets and tracer rounds into the trash pit.

The next morning at sun up, just like clock work, the Gunny went for his morning nature call just as someone was lighting the trash pit on fire to burn what was inside of it. This was a normal practice to get rid of trash. The person who started the fire was from a different unit and had no idea what was in the pit. Just as Gunny dropped his pants to his ankles and sat on the toilet with his back to the trash pit, all the flares started going off into the air, red then green, etc. All of the bullets started going off and buzzing through the air and popping. The Gunny jumped off of the toilet with his pants around his ankles screaming "in coming!" and landed penis first into the sand. We all were laughing so hard we were crying. Gunny did not think it was too funny.

Shortly after that incident I got stuck on a working party to go back to the old oil field barracks we used to shower in six months ago. I had to assist in cleaning every HMMV and truck the Marine Corps had over there. We worked from five in the afternoon until six a.m. the next morning. We had to punch holes in all the floorboards with screwdrivers and hammers and completely rinse all the sand and other debris out of the vehicles. Then they would be inspected to make sure they were spotless, otherwise they would not be able to ship them back to the U.S. What a job that was!

That working party lasted for two long weeks. I finally returned to my unit back at base camp out in the middle of the desert. Where I was exactly I could not tell you. I never knew myself. Upon arriving back at camp we received great news. We were finally going to catch the big freedom bird out of there back to the real world! We spent the next several days tearing down the base camp. We tore down canvass tents, the outhouses we built, filled in all of the pits for burning trash, got rid of excess baggage and packed everything away. We just sat out in the sand and waited.

First, they told us it would be the next day. Then, when morning arrived we were told it would not be until the afternoon. When the bus did not show up that afternoon, we were told it would be the next day. Finally, three long tortuous days later, the bus showed up. The last time I was that excited was when it was the last day of school before summer vacation. It felt so good to be going home. Everyone was so excited on the bus. The bus had been converted to carry stretchers full of wounded people. They expected so many casualties on our side they converted all kinds of Saudi buses and vehicles into ambulances.

We were all talking a mile a minute and so loud as if we were trying to speak over each other. Just like all the kids on that last bus ride home of the school year just before summer vacation. We finally arrived at these barracks in the middle of a bustling town. I still cannot recall what town it was or where it was. I guess they thought we did not need to know. Besides, I did not really care. I was going home.

They told us we would probably be here for a few days until we got a flight out of here. "Gee, that figures. Where have I heard that before?" We settled into our rooms. They had four bunks in them with mattresses and now sheets. There were some wall lockers also. We all then proceeded to take showers. We finally had hot water and soap. We all had forgotten what it was like to really be clean and smell nice. I felt like a snake that had just shed off his old skin after a long winter. I felt like a completely new man. After that, all we had to do was wait.

I found out they had phones here, so I ran over to the phones and called my mom. I told her where I thought I was and that I would be home soon. I made arrangements for her to bring the girl Meggan I had been writing for the past six months. I could not wait to see everyone. As I was getting off of the phone my mom said to be careful. I said, "Don't worry mom the war is over, nothing will happen now. Besides, I'm in a barracks in the middle of town somewhere close to the airport." We then said our goodbyes. I started walking back to my room thinking about how great it was going to be to get home, see my family, the girl Meggan I had been writing, and to party.

I was so excited my stomach got upset. It was like the time I went to my first high school dance with a girl. I was so excited, but nervous at the same time. It felt like I had a thousand butterflies in my stomach. Crack, crack, crack! Out of nowhere I heard shots by the front gate, which I was near. I hit the deck. I had my rifle, but they already took our ammo back. People started running around. I waited there to see what was going to happen. I figured since I did not have ammo I would have to use my knife. So I laid there and waited, thinking I would use the element of surprise to my advantage if any Arabs came through the gate. I waited for about ten minutes and nothing happened. I thought to my self, "What an emotional roller coaster. Is this shit ever going to end? I am getting shot at right until the day I leave. A minute ago I was all excited like a teenager going to his first high school dance with a girl and the next minute my hands are sweaty, my heart pounding and my senses alert. I was ready to carve someone a new asshole. How could I shift gears so fast?" I felt so drained. I finally got up and went back to the barracks. I found out when I got back that there was a drive by with Arabs shooting at us. I thought to myself, "No shit, I think I figured that one out!"

Finally, our big day came and we all loaded onto a bus and headed out to the airport. We got there and sat on the tarmac by a building most of the day and they came by and told us we would not be leaving today. So we got back on the bus and headed back to the barracks. "Why the fuck can't these assholes get their fucking shit together? What is so fucking hard about scheduling a mother-fucking plane to take us home?" Everyone was so angry. We were all cussing and yelling. They just had to keep messing with us right up until the last minute. They just could not let things be and let us go home peacefully.

Finally, again, they loaded us up back onto the bus and drove us to the airport. When we got there we all got into formation and emptied our duffel bags and we were searched by customs to make sure we cleaned everything and did not have any Iraqi weapons. After that crap was over we loaded onto a huge 747 from Hawaiian airlines. We had three airline stewards and one stewardess. Everyone was complaining because all the stewards seemed to be gay and the stewardess was a huge fat lady. Then, to top it off on the movie screen they played "9 $\frac{1}{2}$ weeks". It was a steamy movie with a lot of sexual connotations. "Son-of-a-bitch! They even have to fuck with us on the damn plane. We haven't even seen women in a year and they're going to play this movie and it will at least be eighteen hours before we even land back in California! Well, at least we could smoke on the plane!"

We stopped in Bangor, Maine, and they let us off the plane. We walked down a red carpet that was bordered by a gold rope, kind of like the ones they have at the movie theater preventing you from entering until the pizza faced high school punk decides to unlatch it and let you in. The red carpet led right into the airport bar. There were hundreds of people there. They were all cheering for us. I was numb. It was like a dream. Several hours ago I was in the worst place I have ever been in my life and now all of sudden I am in an airport and people are applauding me for suffering for a year.

I ignored it. All I could think about is getting to the bar. I decided that I would buy four beers at once and pound them. So, I did. Before you know it, I am smashed. There are all kinds of girls in the bar wanting autographs. I signed shirts, butts, breasts, you name it, I signed it. I felt like a puppet in a show. "Do these people really know what I just went through?" I just wanted to get home and be left alone.

We finally got back on the plane and headed for home, sunny California. We all were planning to go to the beach, get ripped and ask every girl we saw to have sex with us. That is all we wanted to do.

Born in the U.S.A.

We finally landed and I would meet my future ex-wife Meggan and be reintroduced to my family. I say this because I had been turned into someone else. I was a blood thirsty killer. I knew nothing except how to survive. I could survive anywhere, anyplace, anytime. I was an animal. I have lived in my own filth, lived with death, smelled death's fowl odor, I have eaten things that would make a boar puke, I have puked, I have killed, I have given my soul for freedom.

I was nothing but a shell filled with death, hate and despair and was about to be unleashed into the real world. "Will my parents still care for me? Will they like me? Will my family and friends still love me? Awe fuck it. I don't give a shit." I no longer knew love. I only knew survival and that only the fittest will win. As I walked off the bus onto the concrete and saw my family and future ex-wife waiting for me another passage from the bible passed through my mind. It is a passage from Job 30:9.

> And now their sons mock me in song; I have become a byword among them. They detest me and keep their distance; they do not hesitate to spit in my face. Now that God has unstrung my bow and afflicted me, they throw off restraint in my presence. On my right the tribe attacks; they lay snares for my feet, they build their siege ramps against me. They break up my road; they succeed in destroying me without anyone's helping them. They advance as through a gaping breach; amid the ruins they come rolling in. Terrors overwhelm me; my dignity is driven away as by the wind, my safety vanishes like a cloud. And now my life ebbs away; days of suffering grip me. Night pierces my bones; my gnawing pains never rest. In his real

power God becomes like clothing to me; he binds me like the neck of my garment. He throws me into the mud, and I am reduced to dust and ashes. I cry out to you, O God, but you do not answer; I stand up, but you merely look at me. You turn on me ruthlessly; with the might of your hand you attack me. You snatch me up and drive me before the wind; you toss me about in the storm. I know you will bring me down to death, to the place appointed for all the living. Surely no one lays a hand on a broken man when he cries for help in his distress. Have I not wept for those in trouble? Has not my soul grieved for the poor? Yet when I hoped for good, evil came; when I looked for light, then came darkness. The churning inside me never stops; days of suffering confront me. I go about blackened, but not by the sun; I stand up in the assembly and cry for help. I have become a brother of jackals, a companion of owls. My skin grows black and peels; my body burns with fever. My harp is tuned to mourning, and my flute to the sound of wailing.

It felt weird to see my family. It was like I was going through the motions, but I was not really there. It still felt like I was in a dream and none of this was really happening. I felt like I had never met these people before. It seemed like I was a foster child from a foreign country just meeting my host parents for the first time. Even though I had my family, friends and hundreds of other people around me, I truly felt alone. I became scared when my fellow Marines left me to go their own separate ways. I had lived like an animal with them for nearly a year. I had been to hell and back with them. Now we were separated. I wanted to be back with them, instead of my family. They knew me. They were just like I was.

When we got back to California I had a year left in the Marine Corps. During that year I got married to Meggan and divorced. I was sent to Regimental Sniper School and graduated first in the class. The government sent eighteen hundred Marines from Camp Pendleton into Los Angeles for the Rodney King riots and right before I got out, Marines were starting to get shipped off to Somalia. However, they let me get out of the Corps so that I could go home.

13
FULL CIRCLE

I look at the empty martini glass I had set on the counter when I got up from my sofa chair and went into the kitchen after reflecting on my experiences. I then picked up that glass and set it into the dishwasher. I return to the family room and my chair. I sit down and begin to think again. I remember moving to Michigan when I got out of the Marines and living with my dad. I remember him telling me I was a "bigger asshole now than when I left".

My ex-wife coaxed me into thinking she was pregnant with my child. I moved all the way across the country back to Arizona to be with her and take care of my responsibilities. I helped deliver the baby, I cut the umbilical cord, I held her hand, and I held the baby. I watched as the doctors botched the episiotomies and blood squirted half way across the room from the arteries they cut. I looked at the placenta in the stainless steel pan. I cried. Two weeks later I took her to get a blood transfusion. Within days after that, she called and told me the baby was not mine. She said she did it just to piss me off and I never heard from her again. I wanted to die. Life sucked. I was surrounded by misery, hate and evil. I drank.

I remember the days when I did not want to live anymore. Friends would ask me, "How was your day?" I would just reply, "It's just another fucking day!" I would then grab a beer and go to my room and get plowed trying to numb myself and escape reality. I was trying to bring myself one more day closer to death. I wanted out of this world. I would think about how evil this world was and the horrible things it made me do all in the name of righteousness. I drank.

I remember getting kicked out of my parents house and living in the back of my truck. I lost all of my friends. My family did not want to be around me because I was so mean that no one could stand me. I got a job as a waiter and saved enough money to rent a room in a house that was infested with crystal meth and pot. I watched a mother do drug deals in front of her one year old baby. I drank.

I recall many bar fights where I cleared out the entire bar after getting drunk and starting my own war because there was no war to fight. I remember people not hiring me for jobs because I could kill a man with a spoon in two seconds. I remember getting thrown in jail because my girlfriend, at that time, told the cops I was holding her down on the bed and beating her. It was all a lie. The police arrived and rattled off my entire military record. The cop told me that it was an impressive record, but they were taking me to jail because of what I had been through and it was a risk to leave me there with her. I drank.

I remember being at lunch with my mother. A waitress walked behind me and dropped some trays on the floor. I flew under the table. After I realized what had happened I got up off the floor and sat back in my chair. Everyone was looking at me. I began to shake and I told my mother we needed to leave. I drank.

I remember being scared of the dark at age twenty-six and not being able to sleep because there was no one on fire watch to guard me at night. I remember lying in bed sweating and trembling. I remember my mind replaying the war in my mind like a tape recorder while I slept. I would wake up in a pool of my own sweat and I would shake. I would cry. I would not go back to sleep. I drank.

I remember driving home from school and having a flashback in the middle of the street while I was still operating the vehicle. It was nighttime and a streetlight had caught my eye and it made me relive the time when the Saudi man had his AK47 nestled in my gut. As I came out of it, I realized that I had come to a complete stop in the middle of the street. I started to shake as I drove the rest of the way home. I drank.

I remember having to sit in corners in class at college and in restaurants. I remember having to sleep against a wall so that it would resemble my fighting hole in the desert. I remember not being able to leave the house because I was afraid. I remember not being able to go to a movie because I was scared of the dark, I would panic and run out of the theater. I drank.

I remember smelling things that resembled the smell of death and I would puke. Then I would shake. I remember hiding on veteran's holidays. I remember looking at my uniform, crying and shaking. I remember staying away from the beach because of all the sand. I remember people asking me questions. I would start to cry and shake. I drank.

I remember being alone, unloved by other human beings, because they thought I was a freak. I remember being ridiculed by people for what I had done. I remember Vietnam vets ridiculing me because I had received a good welcome home and they did not. I remember being told that my war was an easy war and that no one really fought. I remember being told that the Gulf War was not really a war because so few people lost their lives. I drank.

As all of these horrible memories flew through my mind I began to cry again. I was sitting there, still all alone, and I was reminded of a song by Huey Lewis and the News.

Sometimes in my bed at night I curse the dark and I pray for the light and sometimes the lights don't constellation. Blinded if by memory, afraid of what it might do to me and the tears and the sweat only mock my desperation. Don't you know me I am the boy next door. The one you found so easy to ignore. Is that what I was fighting for"? No! Walking on a thin line straight off the front lines labeled as freaks loose on the streets of the city. Walking on a thin line angry all of the time. Take a look at my face. See what its done to me. Taught me how to shoot to kill. A specialist with a deadly skill. A skill that I needed to have to be a survivor. Well it's over now, so they say. Well, sometimes it don't work out that way. Because your never the same when you've been under fire, no!

During those ten years of my life after the war, I had fought many battles trying to be human and trying to rebuild myself. The first four years I did nothing but suffer. I abused myself. I lost everything I had, and hit rock bottom. Luckily for me, my parents and friends tried one more time to help me out. They talked me into going to school.

I put myself through college. I received a Bachelors degree in Anthropology with an emphasis on Archaeology from Arizona State University. While going to school full time, I worked two jobs and did volunteer work on the weekends so that I could network. I did not want to fail. I could not fail. A Marine would complete his mission no matter what the cost. It cost me several thousand dollars and, because I was working so hard, a trip to the hospital when my heart stopped beating for a minute due to the fact that I had just recovered from valley fever, which left me so dehydrated that two I.V. bags did not fully rehydrate me.

While I was completing my college degree I had acquired a job working for the City of Phoenix at a local museum. Eventually, after five years, I worked my way up from cleaning toilets and taking admission fees to the position of Assistant Archaeologist to the City of Phoenix Archaeologist. During that time is when I began the task of writing this book and now I have completed that.

I have patched things up with my family and friends. I have rebuilt myself into a productive part of society. I decide that maybe it is just my lot in life to be alone and I accept it. I have a much higher purpose. I must teach the world what I know. I must try to help, so all of this has not been done in vain.

The war is over for me now. It feels good to say that and mean it. The painful memories filled my soul and had taken it over so that nothing else could get in. Now I can fill my soul with love, peace, and happiness.

A cycle of my life has ended and a new one begins. Just as the sun sets and rises throughout all of its cycles, so do I. I begin to smile. I have made it. I finally made it. I am human again. I can care. I can love. I can live! Nothing in my life will ever be as bad as this. I will be ok. I realize that these experiences will be invaluable to me because no matter what happens to me now I can always say, "I have seen a lot worse!"

Semper Fidelis
Always faithful to your GOD,
Your Country,
and your Corps!

EPILOGUE

After going through the war, rebuilding myself and finally starting a successful career, I realized there are a lot of people in America who just do not get it. They do not really know what America is about. My experience has taught me this. Now a days, most Americans say, "Give me, give me, give me, what are you going to give me?" Yet, someone from a foreign country comes to America and says, "What can I do to better myself and become successful." This is my point. America is about OPPORTUNITY! You can become or achieve anything you want here, as long as you are willing to work for it, no matter what your background is, or what the circumstances are. This is what I believe I was fighting for. This is what I, as a Marine, was protecting...FREEDOM.

As a nation we need to realize that sometimes war is necessary. While we may have control over the actions we as Americans take, we do not have control over other countries and their actions. This reality came home on September 11, 2001 in New York City when the twin towers were destroyed and in Washington D.C. where the Pentagon was partially destroyed by airplanes full of Americans held prisoner by psychotic terrorists. We need the deterrent, called war. Sometimes we need to wage war in all its ferocity.

If we have to go to war we need to be decisive in our actions and unambiguous in our plans. This will help to facilitate our success so that we may expedite the return of our brave men and women. We need to use everything we have at our disposal and eradicate the enemy. War is not politically correct. War is death, pain, suffering, blood, guts, pieces of bodies, stench, vomit, dysentery, starvation, fear, sleeplessness, lawlessness, and power. War is black and white, you live or you die. Politics have no place in war. My point is that politicians should not be directing how we fight wars; the warriors who have fought them should manage wars.

The people we send to fight wars, especially those on the front lines, need the best equipment, weapons, food and water we can provide. They are under enough stress as it is and they do not need the government giving them weapons to test out in the middle of a war. They need weapons that they can be certain will work. The warriors do not need the government testing out new drugs on them to see what effects they have on the human body. The warriors who are in combat need to be well fed and nourished, so that they can win the war. Our government should be helping them not hindering them. War is serious, it is not a game played with human lives.

This is only one piece of war, my own personal experience. My war was only one small part in the entire puzzle. We must remember that, those who fight are the ones who pay the price of war. It is as if your mind is the foundation of the home we sentiens call your body. Your brain is likened to a house payment. You pay that bill the rest of your life. You accept the fact you will always have that payment and you deal with it the best you can. You have a decision to make. Do

Epilogue

you want to work hard and make your house payment in order to keep your home and try to work harder and harder each month to achieve your goals to live a successful happy life. Or, do you decide this task is much too insurmountable and give up, losing everything you once wished for. I have had a home for several years now. Each year I work harder and subsequently I have overcome many battles making my foundation and thus my home, a framework of interdependent principles comprised of a settled organizational pattern. That is why I would like to propose that in the dictionary under the word "war", the definition should read: "The ultimate sacrifice, which lasts for eternity; the most profound display of unselfishness by the soldiers who fight it that mankind will ever witness." Therefore, they once gave up everything they were and had, only to return home with nothing, to fight a battle they were never counseled to face.

The first Gulf War ended with stopping any further advancement of Saddam Hussein's troops into Saudi Arabia and with relieving him and his troops of their occupation of Kuwait. However, we left the sadistic dictator in power. We were ordered to "go home". Now, thirteen years later Saddam Hussein has reared his ugly head again and we are thrown into another war on terrorism.

Saddam Hussein has now been captured. Our government is calling the war a success. While the capture of Saddam has provided some closure for me, it is much too soon to be calling the war a success.

While I do agree that something needs to be done about terrorism, it seems that our government has still not learned its lessons from previous wars such as Vietnam. The capture of Saddam will not end this war. Yes, he aided the terrorists, but he is not the nucleus behind terrorism. We need to expel "terrorism".

A Line In the Sand

Our government fights wars like doctors treat medical conditions. A person goes to a doctor for a problem with diabetes. The doctor prescribes a pill that masks the symptoms and makes the patient feel better. Thus, the patient thinks the doctor is great and has taken care of the problem. What actually should have happened is that the doctor should have told the patient that they needed to go on a diet, lose weight and begin a serious exercise program, which would dissipate the problem with diabetes and therefore, make the patient a much healthier and happier person.

This is exactly what our government has done with Saddam. His capture is the "magic pill" that will mask the effects of our disease and thus persuade us into thinking we now have success. We do not. We will be occupying Iraq for a long time to come. We will end up with a permanent base there. It will be just like the occupation of Korea and the 38th parallel.

Finally, the Arabic people have been fighting since the time of Christ. This is a mindset that these people have always had. The mindset is what we need to change if this is going to be a success. Therefore, we will have to breed this ideology out of these people and that will take at least three generations, if not more. I have closure now because I have finished my book and Saddam has been captured. However, this war will not end for a long, long time.

This is one of the Amtracks that we rode in when we were in Desert Shield (August–December, 1990).

Robert Serocki, Jr., back from patrol in December, 1990. We were guarding a Hawk missile site for the Army.

249

Inside the Amtrack (September–October, 1990)

Wild camel in Saudi Arabia (September, 1990)

Getting ready to move out for the day in the Amtracks (October, 1990).

Robert Serocki, Jr. (on the left) eating breakfast with the Lieutenant (center) and one of his squad leaders (second from right).

The whole platoon, with a Kuwait flag after the war, in base camp (March, 1991)

Us, training to assault a mine field and bunker complex (September–October, 1990).

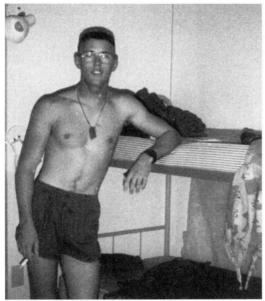

Robert Serocki, Jr., inside the oil field barracks where we took showers once a month during Desert Shield (1990).

Gas mask training, October, 1990 while it was 130°. We had to wear these throughout the day in order to get used to it. We were expecting to get gassed during the war.

Robert Serocki, Jr., with his first Pepsi®—December, 1990 at the Hawk missile site.

Robert Serocki, Jr., telling his family about the plane ride home (March 30, 1991 at Camp Pendleton, California).

My very good friend "Goose" (on the left). This is after the war (March, 1991).

Robert Serocki, Jr., drinking coffee to stay warm after a three-day rain storm in January, 1991.

Football game in the Saudi Desert

My graduation picture from boot camp (December 23, 1988)

Base camp, where we waited in March, 1991 to be taken to the airport to go home.